M
INVENTIONS

MY INVENTIONS

NIKOLA TESLA

Throughout the text readers may find that some of the language used and sentiments expressed are offensive and unacceptable by today's standards. These reflect the attitudes and usage common at the time the book was written. In no way do they reflect the attitude of the publishers.

This edition published in 2025 by Arcturus Publishing Limited
26/27 Bickels Yard, 151–153 Bermondsey Street,
London SE1 3HA

Typesetting by Palimpsest Book Production Limited

Cover design: Peter Ridley
Cover illustration: Peter Gray

AD006599US

Printed in China

FSC
www.fsc.org
MIX
Paper | Supporting responsible forestry
FSC® C104723

Contents

Introduction

Nikola Tesla was born on 10 July 1856 in what is now Smiljan, Croatia, then part of the Austro-Hungarian Empire. While Tesla's father, Milutin Tesla, was a priest for the Serbian Orthodox Church and wished for Tesla to join the priesthood, it was Tesla's mother, Djuka Mandic, who inspired Tesla's interest in invention thanks to her hobby of inventing small household appliances.

During the 1870s, Tesla studied at the Austrian Polytechnic School in Graz but later dropped out due to a gambling problem. It was not long before he continued his education in Prague, attending lectures at the Karl-Ferdinand University. Once he graduated, he began working as Chief Electrician for the Budapest Telephone Exchange. There, he started to tinker with the company's equipment and drew up his first plan of the alternating current (AC) induction motor, after purportedly experiencing a vision. Later, he demonstrated newly-completed versions to various investors, who at first were unaware of its scientific importance.

Determined to prove the worth of his new innovation, Tesla left Europe to find employment in America. It was there that he worked for Thomas Edison, who was impressed by Tesla's skill. But before long a rivalry began between the two inventors. After Edison reneged on a deal, Tesla was only too happy to leave the company. In 1888, he sold his patents for the AC induction motor to George Westinghouse, which propelled him to future achievements.

Tesla included the most notable ones in his 1919 autobiography *My Inventions*, originally published as a series of articles in the scientific magazine *Electrical Experimenter*. This autobiography is a fascinating insight into six pivotal moments in Tesla's life, showcasing the processes, constructions, and applications of his life-changing ingenuities and solidifying him as one of the greatest scientific minds of all time.

Despite Tesla's groundbreaking advancements in science, he died a poor man at the age of 86 in 1943, after the closure of his free energy project caused him to suffer a nervous breakdown. Never seriously considered for the Nobel Prize, despite his exceptional achievements, he is perhaps better understood today than he was in his own time. Tesla's legacy is still evident and his contributions have inspired not just those working in the sciences, but also in many other areas of society.

Chapter 1

My Early Life

The progressive development of man is vitally dependent on invention. It is the most important product of his creative brain. Its ultimate purpose is the complete mastery of mind over the material world, the harnessing of the forces of nature to human needs. This is the difficult task of the inventor who is often misunderstood and unrewarded. But he finds ample compensation in the pleasing exercises of his powers and in the knowledge of being one of that exceptionally privileged class without whom the race would have long ago perished in the bitter struggle against pitiless elements.

Speaking for myself, I have already had more than my full measure of this exquisite enjoyment, so much that for many years my life was little short of continuous rapture. I am credited with being one of the hardest workers and perhaps I am, if thought is the equivalent of labor, for I have devoted to it almost all of my waking hours. But if work is interpreted to be a definite performance in a specified time according to a rigid rule, then I may be the worst of idlers. Every effort under compulsion demands a sacrifice of life-energy. I never paid such a price. On the contrary, I have thrived on my thoughts.

In attempting to give a connected and faithful account of my activities in this series of articles which will be presented with the assistance of the Editors of the *Electrical Experimenter* and are chiefly addressed to our young men readers, I must dwell, however reluctantly, on the impressions of my youth and the circumstances and events which have been instrumental in determining my career.

Our first endeavors are purely instinctive, promptings of an imagination vivid and undisciplined. As we grow older reason asserts itself and we become more and more systematic and designing. But those early impulses, although not immediately productive, are of the greatest moment and may shape our very destinies. Indeed, I feel now that had I understood and cultivated instead of suppressing them, I would have added substantial value to my bequest to the world. But not until I had attained manhood did I realize that I was an inventor.

This was due to a number of causes. In the first place I had a brother who was gifted to an extraordinary degree—one of those rare phenomena of mentality which biological investigation has failed to explain. His premature death left my parents disconsolate. We owned a horse which had been presented to us by a dear friend. It was a magnificent animal of Arabian breed, possessed almost human intelligence, and was cared for and petted by the whole family, having on one occasion saved my father's life under remarkable circumstances. My father had been called one winter night to perform an urgent duty and while crossing the mountains, infested by wolves, the horse became frightened and ran away, throwing him violently to the ground. It arrived home bleeding and exhausted, but after the alarm was sounded immediately dashed off again, returning to the spot, and before the searching party were far on the way they were met by my father, who had recovered consciousness and remounted, not realizing that he had been lying in the snow for several hours. This horse was responsible for my brother's injuries from which he died. I witnessed the tragic scene and although 56 years have elapsed since, my visual impression of it has lost none of its force. The recollection of his attainments made every effort of mine seem dull in comparison.

Anything I did that was creditable merely caused my parents to feel their loss more keenly. So I grew up with little confidence in myself. But I was far from being considered a stupid boy, if I am to judge from an incident of which I have still a strong remembrance. One day the Aldermen were passing through a street where I was at play with other boys. The oldest of these venerable gentlemen—a wealthy citizen—paused to give a silver piece to each of us. Coming to me he suddenly stopped and commanded, "Look in my eyes." I met his gaze, my hand outstretched to receive the much valued coin, when, to my dismay, he said, "No, not much, you can get nothing from me, you are too smart." They used to tell a funny story about me. I had two old aunts with wrinkled faces, one of them having two teeth protruding like the tusks of an elephant which she buried in my cheek every time she kissed me. Nothing would scare me more than the prospect of being hugged by these as affectionate as unattractive relatives. It happened that while being carried in my mother's arms they asked me who was the prettier of the two. After examining their faces intently, I answered thoughtfully, pointing to one of them, "This here is not as ugly as the other."

Then again, I was intended from my very birth for the clerical profession and this thought constantly oppressed me. I longed to be an engineer but my father was inflexible. He was the son of an officer who served in the army of the Great Napoleon and, in common with his brother, professor of mathematics in a prominent institution, had received a military education but, singularly enough, later embraced the clergy in which vocation he achieved eminence. He was a very erudite man, a veritable natural philosopher, poet and writer and his sermons were said to be as eloquent as those of Abraham a Sancta Clara. He had a prodigious memory and frequently recited at length from works in several languages. He often remarked playfully that if some of the classics were lost he could restore them. His style of writing was much admired. He penned sentences short and terse and was full of wit and satire. The humorous remarks he made were always peculiar and characteristic. Just to illustrate, I may mention one or two instances. Among the help there was a cross-eyed man called Mane, employed to do work around the farm. He was chopping wood one day. As he swung the axe my father, who stood nearby and felt very uncomfortable, cautioned him, "For God's sake, Mane, do not strike at what you are looking but at what you intend to hit." On another occasion he was taking out for a drive a friend who carelessly permitted his costly fur coat to rub on the carriage wheel. My father reminded him of it saying, "Pull in your coat, you are ruining my tire." He had the odd habit of talking to himself and would often carry on an animated conversation and indulge in heated argument, changing the tone of his voice. A casual listener might have sworn that several people were in the room.

Although I must trace to my mother's influence whatever inventiveness I possess, the training he gave me must have been helpful. It comprised all sorts of exercises, such as guessing one another's thoughts, discovering the defects of some form or expression, repeating long sentences or performing mental calculations. These daily lessons were intended to strengthen memory and reason and especially to develop the critical sense, and were undoubtedly very beneficial.

My mother descended from one of the oldest families in the country and a line of inventors. Both her father and grandfather originated numerous implements for household, agricultural and other uses. She was a truly great woman, of rare skill, courage and fortitude, who had braved the storms of life and past through many a trying experience. When she was 16 years old a virulent pestilence swept the country. Her father was called away to administer the last sacraments to the dying and during his absence she went alone to the assistance of a neighboring family who were stricken by the dread disease. All of the members, five in number, succumbed in rapid succession. She bathed, clothed and laid out the bodies, decorating them with flowers according to the custom of the country and when her father returned he found everything ready for a Christian burial. My mother was an inventor of the first order and would, I believe, have achieved great things had she not been so remote from modern life and its multi-fold opportunities. She invented and constructed all kinds of tools and devices and wove the finest designs from thread which was spun by her. She even planted the seeds, raised the plants and separated the fibers herself. She worked indefatigably, from break of day till late at night, and most of the wearing apparel and furnishings of the home was the product of her hands. When she was past 60 years old, her fingers were still nimble enough to tie three knots in an eyelash.

There was another and still more important reason for my late awakening. In my boyhood I suffered from a peculiar affliction due to the appearance of images, often accompanied by strong flashes of light, which marred the sight of real objects and interfered with my thought and action. They were pictures of things and scenes which I had really seen, never of those I imagined. When a word was spoken to me the image of the object it designated would present itself vividly to my vision and sometimes I was quite unable to distinguish whether what I saw was tangible or not. This caused me great discomfort and anxiety. None of the students of psychology or physiology whom I have consulted could ever explain satisfactorily these phenomena. They seem to have been unique although I was probably predisposed as I know that my brother experienced a similar trouble. The theory I have formulated is that the images were the result of a reflex action from the brain on the retina under great excitation. They certainly were not hallucinations such as are produced in diseased and anguished minds, for in other respects I was normal and composed. To give an idea of my distress, suppose that I had witnessed a funeral or some such nerve-racking spectacle. Then, inevitably, in the stillness of night, a vivid picture of the scene would thrust itself before my eyes and persist despite all my efforts to banish it. Sometimes it would even remain fixed in space though I pushed my hand through it. If my explanation is correct, it should be able to project on a screen the image of any object one conceives and make it visible. Such an advance would revolutionize all human relations. I am convinced that this wonder can and will be accomplished in time to come; I may add that I have devoted much thought to the solution of the problem.

To free myself of these tormenting appearances, I tried to concentrate my mind on something else I had seen, and in this way I would often obtain temporary relief; but in order to get it I had to conjure continuously new images. It was not long before I found that I had exhausted all of those at my command; my "reel" had run out, as it were, because I had seen little of the world—only objects in my home and the immediate surroundings. As I performed these mental operations for the second or third time, in order to chase the appearances from my vision, the remedy gradually lost all its force. Then I instinctively commenced to make excursions beyond the limits of the small world of which I had knowledge, and I saw new scenes. These were at first very blurred and indistinct, and would flit away when I tried to concentrate my attention upon them, but by and by I succeeded in fixing them; they gained in strength and distinctness and finally assumed the concreteness of real things. I soon discovered that my best comfort was attained if I simply went on in my vision farther and farther, getting new impressions all the time, and so I began to travel—of course, in my mind. Every night (and sometimes during the day), when alone, I would start on my journeys—see new places, cities and countries—live there, meet people and make friendships and acquaintances and, however unbelievable, it is a fact that they were just as dear to me as those in actual life and not a bit less intense in their manifestations.

This I did constantly until I was about 17 years old when my thoughts turned seriously to invention. Then I observed to my delight that I could visualize with the greatest facility. I needed no models, drawings or experiments. I could picture them all as real in my mind. Thus I have been led unconsciously to evolve what I consider a new method of materializing inventive concepts and ideas, which is radically opposite to the purely experimental and is in my opinion ever so much more expeditious and efficient. The moment one constructs a device to carry into practice a crude idea he finds himself unavoidably engrossed with the details and defects of the apparatus. As he goes on improving and reconstructing, his force of concentration diminishes and he loses sight of the great underlying principle. Results may be obtained but always at the sacrifice of quality.

My method is different. I do not rush into actual work. When I get an idea I start at once building it up in my imagination. I change the construction, make improvements and operate the device in my mind. It is absolutely immaterial to me whether I run my turbine in thought or test it in my shop. I even note if it is out of balance. There is no difference whatever, the results are the same. In this way I am able to rapidly develop and perfect a conception without touching anything. When I have gone so far as to embody in the invention every possible improvement I can think of and see no fault anywhere, I put into concrete form this final product of my brain. Invariably my device works as I conceived that it should, and the experiment comes out exactly as I planned it. In 20 years there has not been a single exception. Why should it be otherwise? Engineering, electrical and mechanical, is positive in results. There is scarcely a subject that cannot be mathematically treated and the effects calculated or the results determined beforehand from the available theoretical and practical data. The carrying out into practice of a crude idea as is being generally done is, I hold, nothing but a waste of energy, money and time.

My early affliction had, however, another compensation. The incessant mental exertion developed my powers of observation and enabled me to discover a truth of great importance. I had noted that the appearance of images was always preceded by actual vision of scenes under peculiar and generally very exceptional conditions and I was impelled on each occasion to locate the original impulse. After a while this effort grew to be almost automatic and I gained great facility in connecting cause and effect. Soon I became aware, to my surprise, that every thought I conceived was suggested by an external impression. Not only this but all my actions were prompted in a similar way. In the course of time it became perfectly evident to me that I was merely an automaton endowed with power of movement, responding to the stimuli of the sense organs and thinking and acting accordingly. The practical result of this was the art of telautomatics which has been so far carried out only in an imperfect manner. Its latent possibilities will, however, be eventually shown. I have been since years planning self-controlled automata and believe that mechanisms can be produced which will act as if possessed of reason, to a limited degree, and will create a revolution in many commercial and industrial departments.

I was about 12 years old when I first succeeded in banishing an image from my vision by wilful effort, but

I never had any control over the flashes of light to which I have referred. They were, perhaps, my strangest experience and inexplicable. They usually occurred when I found myself in a dangerous or distressing situation, or when I was greatly exhilarated. In some instances I have seen all the air around me filled with tongues of living flame. Their intensity, instead of diminishing, increased with time and seemingly attained a maximum when I was about 25 years old. While in Paris, in 1883, a prominent French manufacturer sent me an invitation to a shooting expedition which I accepted. I had been long confined to the factory and the fresh air had a wonderfully invigorating effect on me. On my return to the city that night I felt a positive sensation that my brain had caught fire. I saw a light as though a small sun was located in it and I past the whole night applying cold compressions to my tortured head. Finally the flashes diminished in frequency and force but it took more than three weeks before they wholly subsided. When a second invitation was extended to me my answer was an emphatic NO!

These luminous phenomena still manifest themselves from time to time, as when a new idea opening up possibilities strikes me, but they are no longer exciting, being of relatively small intensity. When I close my eyes I invariably observe first, a background of very dark and uniform blue, not unlike the sky on a clear but starless night. In a few seconds this field becomes animated with innumerable scintillating flakes of green, arranged in several layers and advancing towards me. Then there appears, to the right, a beautiful pattern of two systems of parallel and closely spaced lines, at right angles to one another, in all sorts of colors with yellow-green and gold predominating. Immediately thereafter the lines grow brighter and the whole is thickly sprinkled with dots of twinkling light. This picture moves slowly across the field of vision and in about ten seconds vanishes to the left, leaving behind a ground of rather unpleasant and inert grey which quickly gives way to a billowy sea of clouds, seemingly trying to mould themselves in living shapes. It is curious that I cannot project a form into this grey until the second phase is reached. Every time, before falling asleep, images of persons or objects flit before my view. When I see them I know that I am about to lose consciousness. If they are absent and refuse to come it means a sleepless night.

To what an extent imagination played a part in my early life I may illustrate by another odd experience. Like most children I was fond of jumping and developed an intense desire to support myself in the air. Occasionally a strong wind richly charged with oxygen blew from the mountains rendering my body as light as cork and then I would leap and float in space for a long time. It was a delightful sensation and my disappointment was keen when later I undeceived myself.

During that period I contracted many strange likes, dislikes and habits, some of which I can trace to external impressions while others are unaccountable. I had a violent aversion against the earrings of women but other ornaments, as bracelets, pleased me more or less according to design. The sight of a pearl would almost give me a fit but I was fascinated with the glitter of crystals or objects with sharp edges and plane surfaces. I would not touch the hair of other people except, perhaps, at the point of a revolver. I would get a fever by looking at a peach and if a piece of camphor was anywhere in the house it caused me the keenest discomfort. Even now I am not insensible to some of these upsetting impulses. When I drop little squares of paper in a dish filled with liquid, I always sense a peculiar and awful taste in my mouth. I counted the steps in my walks and calculated the cubical contents of soup plates, coffee cups and pieces of food—otherwise my meal was unenjoyable. All repeated acts or operations I performed had to be divisible by three and if I mist I felt impelled to do it all over again, even if it took hours.

Up to the age of eight years, my character was weak and vacillating. I had neither courage or strength to form a firm resolve. My feelings came in waves and surges and vibrated unceasingly between extremes. My wishes were of consuming force and like the heads of the hydra, they multiplied. I was oppressed by thoughts of pain in life and death and religious fear. I was swayed by superstitious belief and lived in constant dread of the spirit of evil, of ghosts and ogres and other unholy monsters of the dark. Then, all at once, there came a tremendous change which altered the course of my whole existence. Of all things I liked books the best. My father had a large library and whenever I could manage I tried to satisfy my passion for reading. He did not permit it and would fly into a rage when he caught me in the act. He hid the candles when he found that I was reading in secret. He did not want me to spoil my eyes. But I obtained tallow, made the wicking and cast the sticks into tin forms, and every night I would bush the keyhole and the cracks and read, often till dawn, when all others slept and my mother started on her arduous daily task. On one occasion I came across a novel entitled *Abafi* (the Son of Aba), a Serbian translation of a well known Hungarian writer, Josika. This work somehow awakened my dormant powers of will and I began to practice self-control.

At first my resolutions faded like snow in April, but in a little while I conquered my weakness and felt a pleasure I never knew before—that of doing as I willed. In the course of time this vigorous mental exercise became second nature. At the outset my wishes had to be subdued but gradually desire and will grew to be identical. After years of such discipline I gained so complete a mastery over myself that I toyed with passions which have meant destruction to some of the strongest men.

At a certain age I contracted a mania for gambling which greatly worried my parents. To sit down to a game of cards was for me the quintessence of pleasure. My father led an exemplary life and could not excuse the senseless waste of time and money in which I indulged. I had a strong resolve but my philosophy was bad. I would say to him, "I can stop whenever I please but is it worth while to give up that which I would purchase with the joys of Paradise?" On frequent occasions he gave vent to his anger and contempt but my mother was different. She understood the character of men and knew that one's salvation could only be brought about through his own efforts. One afternoon, I remember, when I had lost all my money and was craving for a game, she came to me with a roll of bills and said, "Go and enjoy yourself. The sooner you lose all we possess the better it will be. I know that you will get over it." She was right. I conquered my passion then and there and only regretted that it had not been a hundred times as strong. I not only vanquished but tore it from my heart so as not to leave even a trace of desire. Ever since that time I have been as indifferent to any form of gambling as to picking teeth.

During another period I smoked excessively, threatening to ruin my health. Then my will asserted itself and I not only stopped but destroyed all inclination. Long ago I suffered from heart trouble until I discovered that it was due to the innocent cup of coffee I consumed every morning. I discontinued at once, although I confess it was not an easy task. In this way I checked and bridled other habits and passions and have not only preserved my life but derived an immense amount of satisfaction from what most men would consider privation and sacrifice.

After finishing the studies at the Polytechnic Institute and University I had a complete nervous breakdown and while the malady lasted I observed many phenomena strange and unbelievable.

Chapter 2

My First Efforts At Invention

I shall dwell briefly on these extraordinary experiences, on account of their possible interest to students of psychology and physiology and also because this period of agony was of the greatest consequence on my mental development and subsequent labors. But it is indispensable to first relate the circumstances and conditions which preceded them and in which might be found their partial explanation.

From childhood I was compelled to concentrate attention upon myself. This caused me much suffering but, to my present view, it was a blessing in disguise for it has taught me to appreciate the inestimable value of introspection in the preservation of life, as well as a means of achievement.

The pressure of occupation and the incessant stream of impressions pouring into our consciousness through all the gateways of knowledge make modern existence hazardous in many ways. Most persons are so absorbed in the contemplation of the outside world that they are wholly oblivious to what is passing on within themselves.

The premature death of millions is primarily traceable to this cause. Even among those who exercise care it is a common mistake to avoid imaginary, and ignore the real dangers. And what is true of an individual also applies, more or less, to a people as a whole.

Witness, in illustration, the prohibition movement. A drastic, if not unconstitutional, measure is now being put through in this country to prevent the consumption of alcohol and yet it is a positive fact that coffee, tea, tobacco, chewing gum and other stimulants, which are freely indulged in even at the tender age, are vastly more injurious to the national body, judging from the number of those who succumb. So, for instance, during my student years I gathered from the published necrologues in Vienna, the home of coffee drinkers, that deaths from heart trouble sometimes reached 67% of the total. Similar observations might probably be made in cities where the consumption of tea is excessive. These delicious beverages super-excite and gradually exhaust the fine fibers of the brain. They also interfere seriously with arterial circulation and should be enjoyed all the more sparingly as their deleterious effects are slow and imperceptible. Tobacco, on the other hand, is conducive to easy and pleasant thinking and detracts from the intensity and concentration necessary to all original and vigorous effort of the intellect. Chewing gum is helpful for a short while but soon drains the glandular system and inflicts irreparable damage, not to speak of the revulsion it creates. Alcohol in small quantities is an excellent tonic, but is toxic in its action when absorbed in larger amounts, quite immaterial as to whether it is taken in as whiskey or produced in the stomach from sugar. But it should not be overlooked that all these are great eliminators assisting Nature, as they do, in upholding her stern but just law of the survival of the fittest. Eager reformers should also be mindful of the eternal perversity of mankind which makes the indifferent "laissez-faire" by far preferable to enforced restraint.

The truth about this is that we need stimulants to do our best work under present living conditions, and that we must exercise moderation and control our appetites and inclinations in every direction. That is what I have been doing for many years, in this way maintaining myself young in body and mind. Abstinence was not always to my liking but I find ample reward in the agreeable experiences I am now making. Just in the hope of converting some to my precepts and convictions I will recall one or two.

A short time ago I was returning to my hotel. It was a bitter cold night, the ground slippery, and no taxi to be had. Half a block behind me followed another man, evidently as anxious as myself to get under cover. Suddenly my legs went up in the air. In the same instant there was a flash in my brain, the nerves responded, the muscles contracted, I swung through 180 degrees and landed on my hands. I resumed my walk as though nothing had happened when the stranger caught up with me. "How old are you?" he asked, surveying me critically. "Oh, about 59," I replied. "What of it?" "Well," said he, "I have seen a cat do this but never a man." About a month since I wanted to order new eyeglasses and went to an oculist who put me through the usual tests. He looked at me incredulously as I read off with ease the smallest print at considerable distance. But when I told him that I was past sixty he gasped in astonishment. Friends of mine often remark that my suits fit me like gloves but they do not know that all my clothing is made to measurements which were taken nearly 35 years ago and never changed. During this same period my weight has not varied one pound.

In this connection I may tell a funny story. One evening, in the winter of 1885, Mr. Edison, Edward H. Johnson, the President of the Edison Illuminating Company, Mr. Batchellor, Manager of the Works, and myself entered a little place opposite 65 Fifth Avenue where the offices of the company were located. Someone suggested guessing weights and I was induced to step on a scale. Edison felt me all over and said: "Tesla weighs 152 lbs. to an ounce," and he guest it exactly. Stripped I weighed 142 lbs. and that is still my weight. I whispered to Mr. Johnson, "How is it possible that Edison could guess my weight so closely?" "Well," he said, lowering his voice. "I will tell you, confidentially, but you must not say anything. He was employed for a long time in a Chicago slaughter-house where he weighed thousands of hogs every day! That's why." My friend, the Honorable Chauncey M. Depew, tells of an Englishman on whom he sprung one of his original anecdotes and who listened with a puzzled expression but—a year later—laughed out loud. I will frankly confess it took me longer than that to appreciate Johnson's joke.

Now, my well-being is simply the result of a careful and measured mode of living and perhaps the most astonishing thing is that three times in my youth I was rendered by illness a hopeless physical wreck and given up by physicians. More than this, through ignorance and light-heartedness, I got into all sorts of difficulties, dangers and scrapes from which I extricated myself as by enchantment. I was almost drowned a dozen times; was nearly boiled alive and just mist being cremated. I was entombed, lost and frozen. I had hair-breadth escapes from mad dogs, hogs, and other wild animals. I past through dreadful diseases and met with all kinds of odd mishaps and that I am hale and hearty today seems like a miracle. But as I recall these incidents to my mind I feel convinced that my preservation was not altogether accidental.

An inventor's endeavor is essentially lifesaving. Whether he harnesses forces, improves devices, or provides new comforts and conveniences, he is adding to the safety of our existence. He is also better qualified than the average individual to protect himself in peril, for he is observant and resourceful. If I had no other evidence that I was, in a measure, possessed of such qualities I would find it in these personal experiences. The reader will be able to judge for himself if I mention one or two instances.

On one occasion, when about 14 years old, I wanted to scare some friends who were bathing with me. My plan was to dive under a long floating structure and slip out quietly at the other end. Swimming and diving came to me as naturally as to a duck and I was confident that I could perform the feat. Accordingly I plunged into the water and, when out of view, turned around and proceeded rapidly towards the opposite side. Thinking that I was safely beyond the structure, I rose to the surface but to my dismay struck a beam. Of course, I quickly dived and forged ahead with rapid strokes until my breath was beginning to give out. Rising for the second time, my head came again in contact with a beam. Now I was becoming desperate. However, summoning all my energy, I made a third frantic attempt but the result was the same. The torture of suppressed breathing was getting unendurable, my brain was reeling and I felt myself sinking. At that moment, when my situation seemed absolutely hopeless, I experienced one of those flashes of light and the structure above me appeared before my vision. I either discerned or guessed that there was a little space between the surface of the water and the boards resting on the beams and, with consciousness nearly gone, I floated up, pressed my mouth close to the planks and managed to inhale a little air, unfortunately mingled with a spray of water which nearly choked me. Several times I repeated this procedure as in a dream until my heart, which was racing at a terrible rate, quieted down and I gained composure. After that I made a number of unsuccessful dives, having completely lost the sense of direction, but finally succeeded in getting out of the trap when my friends had already given me up and were fishing for my body.

That bathing season was spoiled for me through recklessness but I soon forgot the lesson and only two years later I fell into a worse predicament. There was a large flour mill with a dam across the river near the city where I was studying at that time. As a rule the height of the water was only two or three inches above the dam and to swim out to it was a sport not very dangerous in which I often indulged. One day I went alone to the river to enjoy myself as usual. When I was a short distance from the masonry, however, I was horrified to observe that the water had risen and was carrying me along swiftly. I tried to get away but it was too late. Luckily, though, I saved myself from being swept over by taking hold of the wall with both hands. The pressure against my chest was great and I was barely able to keep my head above the surface. Not a soul was in sight and my voice was lost in the roar of the fall. Slowly and gradually I became exhausted and unable to withstand the strain longer. Just as I was about to let go, to be dashed against the rocks below, I saw in a flash of light a familiar diagram illustrating the hydraulic principle that the pressure of a fluid in motion is proportionate to the area exposed, and automatically I turned on my left side. As if by magic the pressure was reduced and I found it comparatively easy in that position to resist the force of the stream. But the danger still confronted me. I knew that sooner or later I would be carried down, as it was not possible for any help to reach me in time, even if I attracted attention. I am ambidextrous now but then I was left-handed and had comparatively little strength in my right arm. For this reason I did not dare to turn on the other side to rest and nothing remained but to slowly push my body along the dam. I had to get away from the mill towards which my face was turned as the current there was much swifter and deeper. It was a long and painful ordeal and I came near to failing at its very end for I was confronted with a depression in the masonry. I managed to get over with the last ounce of my force and fell in a swoon when I reached the bank, where I was found. I had torn virtually all the skin from my left side and it took several weeks before the fever subsided and I was well. These are only two of many instances but they may be sufficient to show that had it not been for the inventor's instinct I would not have lived to tell this tale.

Interested people have often asked me how and when I began to invent. This I can only answer from my present recollection in the light of which the first attempt I recall was rather ambitious for it involved the invention of an apparatus and a method. In the former I was anticipated but the latter was original. It happened in this way. One of my playmates had come into the possession of a hook and fishing-tackle which created quite an excitement in the village, and the next morning all started out to catch frogs. I was left alone and deserted owing to a quarrel with this boy. I had never seen a real hook and pictured it as something wonderful, endowed with peculiar qualities, and was despairing not to be one of the party. Urged by necessity, I somehow got hold of a piece of soft iron wire, hammered the end to a sharp point between two stones, bent it into shape, and fastened it to a strong string. I then cut a rod, gathered some bait, and went down to the brook where there were frogs in abundance. But I could not catch any and was almost discouraged when it occurred to me to dangle the empty hook in front of a frog sitting on a stump. At first he collapsed but by and by his eyes bulged out and became bloodshot, he swelled to twice his normal size and made a vicious snap at the hook. Immediately I pulled him up. I tried the same thing again and again and the method proved infallible. When my comrades, who in spite of their fine outfit had caught nothing, came to me they were green with envy. For a long time I kept my secret and enjoyed the monopoly but finally yielded to the spirit of Christmas. Every boy could then do the same and the following summer brought disaster to the frogs.

In my next attempt I seem to have acted under the first instinctive impulse which later dominated me—to harness the energies of nature to the service of man. I did this through the medium of May-bugs (or June-bugs as they are called in America) which were a veritable pest in that country and sometimes broke the branches of trees by the sheer weight of their bodies. The bushes were black with them. I would attach as many as four of them to a rotor on a thin spindle, and transmit the motion of the same to a large disc and so derive considerable "power." These creatures were remarkably efficient, for once they were started they had no sense to stop and continued whirling for hours and hours and the hotter it was the harder they worked. All went well until a strange boy came to the place. He was the son of a retired officer in the Austrian Army. That urchin ate May-bugs alive and enjoyed them as though they were the finest blue-point oysters. That disgusting sight terminated my endeavors in this promising field and I have never since been able to touch a May-bug or any other insect for that matter.

After that, I believe, I undertook to take apart and assemble the clocks of my grandfather. In the former operation I was always successful but often failed in the latter. So it came that he brought my work to a sudden halt in a manner not too delicate and it took 30 years before I tackled another clockwork again. Shortly there after I went into the manufacture of a kind of pop-gun which comprised a hollow tube, a piston, and two plugs of hemp. When firing the gun, the piston was pressed against the stomach and the tube was pushed back quickly with both hands. The air between the plugs was compressed and raised to high temperature and one of them was expelled with a loud report. The art consisted in selecting a tube of the proper taper from the hollow stalks. I did very well with that gun but my activities interfered with the window panes in our house and met with painful discouragement. If I remember rightly, I then took to carving swords from pieces of furniture which I could conveniently obtain. At that time I was under the sway of the Serbian national poetry and full of admiration for the feats of the heroes. I used to spend hours in mowing down my enemies in the form of corn-stalks which ruined the crops and netted me several spankings from my mother. Moreover these were not of the formal kind but the genuine article.

I had all this and more behind me before I was six years old and had past through one year of elementary school in the village of Smiljan where I was born. At this juncture we moved to the little city of Gospic nearby. This change of residence was like a calamity to me. It almost broke my heart to part from our pigeons, chickens and sheep, and our magnificent flock of geese which used to rise to the clouds in the morning and return from the feeding grounds at sundown in battle formation, so perfect that it would have put a squadron of the best aviators of the present day to shame. In our new house I was but a prisoner, watching the strange people I saw through the window blinds. My bashfulness was such that I would rather have faced a roaring lion than one of the city dudes who strolled about. But my hardest trial came on Sunday when I had to dress up and attend the service. There I meet with an accident, the mere thought of which made my blood curdle like sour milk for years afterwards. It was my second adventure in a church. Not long before I was entombed for a night in an old chapel on an inaccessible mountain which was visited only once a year. It was an awful experience, but this one was worse. There was a wealthy lady in town, a good but pompous woman, who used to come to the church gorgeously painted up and attired with an enormous train and attendants. One Sunday I had just finished ringing the bell in the belfry and rushed downstairs when this grand dame was sweeping out and I jumped on her train. It tore off with a ripping noise which sounded like a salvo of musketry fired by raw recruits. My father was livid with rage. He gave me a gentle slap on the cheek, the only corporal punishment he ever administered to me but I almost feel it now. The embarrassment and confusion that followed are indescribable. I was practically ostracised until something else happened which redeemed me in the estimation of the community.

An enterprising young merchant had organized a fire department. A new fire engine was purchased, uniforms provided and the men drilled for service and parade. The engine was, in reality, a pump to be worked by sixteen men and was beautifully painted red and black. One afternoon the official trial was prepared for and the machine was transported to the river. The entire population turned out to witness the great spectacle. When all the speeches and ceremonies were concluded, the command was given to pump, but not a drop of water came from the nozzle. The professors and experts tried in vain to locate the trouble. The fizzle was complete when I arrived at the scene. My knowledge of the mechanism was nil and I knew next to nothing of air pressure, but instinctively I felt for the suction hose in the water and found that it had collapsed. When I waded in the river and opened it up the water rushed forth and not a few Sunday clothes were spoiled.

Archimedes running naked through the streets of Syracuse and shouting Eureka at the top of his voice did not make a greater impression than myself. I was carried on the shoulders and was the hero of the day.

Upon settling in the city I began a four year course in the so-called Normal School preparatory to my studies at the College or Real Gymnasium. During this period my boyish efforts and exploits, as well as troubles, continued. Among other things I attained the unique distinction of champion crow catcher in the country. My method of procedure was extremely simple. I would go in the forest, hide in the bushes, and imitate the call of the bird. Usually I would get several answers and in a short while a crow would flutter down into the shrubbery near me. After that all I needed to do was to throw a piece of cardboard to distract its attention, jump up and grab it before it could extricate itself from the undergrowth. In this way I would capture as many as I desired. But on one occasion something occurred which made me respect them. I had caught a fine pair of birds and was returning home with a friend. When we left the forest, thousands of crows had gathered making a frightful racket. In a few minutes they rose in pursuit and soon enveloped us. The fun lasted until all of a sudden I received a blow on the back of my head which knocked me down. Then they attacked me viciously. I was compelled to release the two birds and was glad to join my friend who had taken refuge in a cave.

In the schoolroom there were a few mechanical models which interested me and turned my attention to water turbines. I constructed many of these and found great pleasure in operating them. How extraordinary was my life an incident may illustrate. My uncle had no use for this kind of pastime and more than once rebuked me. I was fascinated by a description of Niagara Falls I had perused, and pictured in my imagination a big wheel run by the Falls. I told my uncle that I would go to America and carry out this scheme. Thirty years later I saw my ideas carried out at Niagara and marveled at the unfathomable mystery of the mind.

I made all kinds of other contrivances and contraptions but among these the arbalist I produced were the best. My arrows, when shot, disappeared from sight and at close range traversed a plank of pine 1 inch thick. through the continuous tightening of the bows I developed skin on my stomach very much like that of a crocodile and I am often wondering whether it is due to this exercise that I am able even now to digest cobblestones! Nor can I pass in silence my performances with the sling which would have enabled me to give a stunning exhibit at the Hippodrome.

And now I will tell of one of my feats with this antique implement of war which will strain to the utmost the credulity of the reader. I was practicing while walking with my uncle along the river. The sun was setting, the trout were playful and from time to time one would shoot up into the air, its glistening body sharply defined against a projecting rock beyond. Of course any boy might have hit a fish under these propitious conditions but I undertook a much more difficult task and I foretold to my uncle, to the minutest detail, what I intended doing. I was to hurl a stone to meet the fish, press its body against the rock, and cut it in two. It was no sooner said than done. My uncle looked at me almost scared out of his wits and exclaimed "Vade retro Satanas!" and it was a few days before he spoke to me again. Other records, how ever great, will be eclipsed but I feel that I could peacefully rest on my laurels for a thousand years.

Chapter 3
My Later Endeavors

The Discovery of the Rotating Magnetic Field

At the age of ten I entered the Real Gymnasium which was a new and fairly well equipped institution. In the department of physics were various models of classical scientific apparatus, electrical and mechanical. The demonstrations and experiments performed from time to time by the instructors fascinated me and were undoubtedly a powerful incentive to invention. I was also passionately fond of mathematical studies and often won the Professor's praise for rapid calculation. This was due to my acquired facility of visualizing the figures and performing the operations, not in the usual intuitive manner, but as in actual life. Up to a certain degree of complexity it was absolutely the same to me whether I wrote the symbols on the board or conjured them before my mental vision. But freehand drawing, to which many hours of the course were devoted, was an annoyance I could not endure. This was rather remarkable as most of the members of the family excelled in it. Perhaps my aversion was simply due to the predilection I found in undisturbed thought. Had it not been for a few exceptionally stupid boys, who could not do anything at all, my record would have been the worst. It was a serious handicap as under the then existing educational regime, drawing being obligatory, this deficiency threatened to spoil my whole career and my father had considerable trouble in railroading me from one class to another.

In the second year at that institution I became obsessed with the idea of producing continuous motion through steady air pressure. The pump incident, of which I have told, had set afire my youthful imagination and impress me with the boundless abilities of a vacuum. I grew frantic in my desire to harness this inexhaustible energy but for a long time I was groping in the dark. Finally, however, my endeavors crystallized in an invention which was to enable me to achieve what no other mortal ever attempted.

Imagine a cylinder freely rotatable on two bearings and partly surrounded by a rectangular trough which fits it perfectly. The open side of the trough is closed by a partition so that the cylindrical segment within the enclosure divides the latter into two compartments entirely separated from each other by air-tight sliding joints. One of these compartments being sealed and once for all exhausted, the other remaining open, a perpetual rotation of the cylinder would result, at least, I thought so. A wooden model was constructed and fitted with infinite care and when I applied the pump on one side and actually observed that there was a tendency to turning, I was delirious with joy. Mechanical flight was the one thing I wanted to accomplish although still under the discouraging recollection of a bad fall I sustained by jumping with an umbrella from the top of a building. Every day I used to transport myself through the air to distant regions but could not understand just how I managed to do it. Now I had something concrete—a flying machine with nothing more than a rotating shaft, flapping wings, and a vacuum of unlimited power! From that time on I made my daily aerial excursions in a vehicle of comfort and luxury as might have befitted King Solomon. It took years before I understood that the atmospheric pressure acted at right angles to the surface of the cylinder and that the slight rotary effort I observed was due to a leak. Though this knowledge came gradually it gave me a painful shock.

I had hardly completed my course at the Real Gymnasium when I was prostrated with a dangerous illness or rather, a score of them, and my condition became so desperate that I was given up by physicians. During this period I was permitted to read constantly, obtaining books from the Public Library which had been neglected and entrusted to me for classification of the works and preparation of the catalogues. One day I was handed a few volumes of new literature unlike anything I had ever read before and so captivating as to make me utterly forget my hopeless state. They were the earlier works of Mark Twain and to them might have been due the miraculous recovery which followed. Twenty-five years later, when I met Mr. Clemens and we formed a friendship between us, I told him of the experience and was amazed to see that great man of laughter burst into tears.

My studies were continued at the higher Real Gymnasium in Carlstadt, Croatia, where one of my aunts resided. She was a distinguished lady, the wife of a Colonel who was an old war-horse having participated in many battles. I never can forget the three years I passed at their home. No fortress in time of war was under a more rigid discipline. I was fed like a canary bird. All the meals were of the highest quality and deliciously prepared but short in quantity by a thousand percent. The slices of ham cut by my aunt were like tissue paper. When the Colonel would put something substantial on my plate she would snatch it away and say excitedly to him: "Be careful, Niko is very delicate." I had a voracious appetite and suffered like Tantalus. But I lived in an atmosphere of refinement and artistic taste quite unusual for those times and conditions. The land was low and marshy and malaria fever never left me while there despite of the enormous amounts of quinine I consumed. Occasionally the river would rise and drive an army of rats into the buildings, devouring everything even to the bundles of the fierce paprika. These pests were to me a welcome diversion. I thinned their ranks by all sorts of means, which won me the unenviable distinction of rat-catcher in the community.

At last, however, my course was completed, the misery ended, and I obtained the certificate of maturity which brought me to the cross-roads.

During all those years my parents never wavered in their resolve to make me embrace the clergy, the mere thought of which filled me with dread. I had become intensely interested in electricity under the stimulating influence of my Professor of Physics, who was an ingenious man and often demonstrated the principles by apparatus of his own invention. Among these I recall a device in the shape of a freely rotatable bulb, with tinfoil coatings, which was made to spin rapidly when connected to a static machine. It is impossible for me to convey an adequate idea of the intensity of feeling I experienced in witnessing his exhibitions of these mysterious phenomena. Every impression produced a thousand echoes in my mind. I wanted to know more of this wonderful force; I longed for experiment and investigation and resigned myself to the inevitable with aching heart.

Just as I was making ready for the long journey home I received word that my father wished me to go on a shooting expedition. It was a strange request as he had been always strenuously opposed to this kind of sport. But a few days later I learned that the cholera was raging in that district and, taking advantage of an opportunity, I returned to Gospic in disregard of my parents' wishes. It is incredible how absolutely ignorant people were as to the causes of this scourge which visited the country in intervals of from 15 to 20 years. They thought that the deadly agents were transmitted through the air and filled it with pungent odors and smoke. In the meantime they drank the infected water and died in heaps. I contracted the awful disease on the very day of my arrival and although surviving the crisis, I was confined to bed for nine months with scarcely any ability to move. My energy was completely exhausted and for the second time I found myself at death's door. In one of the sinking spells which was thought to be the last, my father rushed into the room. I still see his pallid face as he tried to cheer me in tones belying his assurance. "Perhaps," I said, "I may get well if you will let me study engineering." "You will go to the best technical institution in the world," he solemnly replied, and I knew that he meant it. A heavy weight was lifted from my mind but the relief would have come too late had it not been for a marvelous cure brought about through a bitter decoction of a peculiar bean. I came to life like another Lazarus to the utter amazement of everybody.

My father insisted that I spend a year in healthful physical outdoor exercises to which I reluctantly consented. For most of this term I roamed in the mountains, loaded with a hunter's outfit and a bundle of books, and this contact with nature made me stronger in body as well as in mind. I thought and planned, and conceived many ideas almost as a rule delusive. The vision was clear enough but the knowledge of principles was very limited. In one of my inventions I proposed to convey letters and packages across the seas, through a submarine tube, in spherical containers of sufficient strength to resist the hydraulic pressure. The pumping plant, intended to force the water through the tube, was accurately figured and designed and all other particulars carefully worked out. Only one trifling detail, of no consequence, was lightly dismissed. I assumed an arbitrary velocity of the water and, what is more, took pleasure in making it high, thus arriving at a stupendous performance supported by faultless calculations. Subsequent reflections, however, on the resistance of pipes to fluid flow determined me to make this invention public property.

Another one of my projects was to construct a ring around the equator which would, of course, float freely and could be arrested in its spinning motion by reactionary forces, thus enabling travel at a rate of about one thousand miles an hour, impracticable by rail. The reader will smile. The plan was difficult of execution, I will admit, but not nearly so bad as that of a well-known New York Professor, who wanted to pump the air from the torrid to the temperate zones, entirely forgetful of the fact that the Lord had provided a gigantic machine for this very purpose.

Still another scheme, far more important and attractive, was to derive power from the rotational energy of terrestrial bodies. I had discovered that objects on the earth's surface, owing to the diurnal rotation of the globe, are carried by the same alternately in and against the direction of translatory movement. From this results a great change in momentum which could be utilized in the simplest imaginable manner to furnish motive effort in any habitable region of the world. I cannot find words to describe my disappointment when later I realized that I was in the predicament of Archimedes, who vainly sought for a fixed point in the universe.

At the termination of my vacation I was sent to the Polytechnic School in Gratz, Styria, which my father had chosen as one of the oldest and best reputed institutions. That was the moment I had eagerly awaited and I began my studies under good auspices and firmly resolved to succeed. My previous training was above the average, due to my father's teaching and opportunities afforded. I had acquired the knowledge of a number of languages and waded through the books of several libraries, picking up information more or less useful. Then again, for the first time, I could choose my subjects as I liked, and free-hand drawing was to bother me no more.

I had made up my mind to give my parents a surprise, and during the whole first year I regularly started my work at three o'clock in the morning and continued until 11 at night, no Sundays or holidays excepted. As most of my fellow-students took things easily, naturally enough I eclipsed all records. In the course of that year I past through nine exams and the professors thought I deserved more than the highest qualifications. Armed with their flattering certificates, I went home for a short rest, expecting a triumph, and was mortified when my father made light of these hard won honors. That almost killed my ambition; but later, after he had died, I was pained to find a package of letters which the professors had written him to the effect that unless he took me away from the Institution I would be killed through overwork.

Thereafter I devoted myself chiefly to physics, mechanics and mathematical studies, spending the hours of leisure in the libraries. I had a veritable mania for finishing whatever I began, which often got me into difficulties. On one occasion I started to read the works of Voltaire when I learned, to my dismay, that there were close on one hundred large volumes in small print which that monster had written while drinking 72 cups of black coffee per diem. It had to be done, but when I laid aside the last book I was very glad, and said, "Never more!"

My first year's showing had won me the appreciation and friendship of several professors. Among these were Prof. Rogner, who was teaching arithmetical subjects and geometry; Prof. Poeschl, who held the chair of theoretical and experimental physics, and Dr. Alle, who taught integral calculus and specialized in differential equations. This scientist was the most brilliant lecturer to whom I ever listened. He took a special interest in my progress and would frequently remain for an hour or two in the lecture room, giving me problems to solve, in which I delighted. To him I explained a flying machine I had conceived, not an illusionary invention, but one based on sound, scientific principles, which has become realizable through my turbine and will soon be given to the world. Both Professors Rogner and Poeschl were curious men. The former had peculiar ways of expressing himself and whenever he did so there was a riot, followed by a long and embarrassing pause. Prof. Poeschl was a methodical and thoroughly grounded German. He had enormous feet and hands like the paws of a bear, but all of his experiments were skillfully performed with clock-like precision and without a miss.

It was in the second year of my studies that we received a Gramme dynamo from Paris, having the horseshoe form of a laminated field magnet, and a wire-wound armature with a commutator. It was connected up and various effects of the currents were shown. While Prof. Poeschl was making demonstrations, running the machine as a motor, the brushes gave trouble, sparking badly, and I observed that it might be possible to operate a motor without these appliances. But he declared that it could not be done and did me the honor of delivering a lecture on the subject, at the conclusion of which he remarked: "Mr. Tesla may accomplish great things, but he certainly never will do this. It would be equivalent to converting a steadily pulling force, like that of gravity, into a rotary effort. It is a perpetual motion scheme, an impossible idea." But instinct is something which transcends knowledge. We have, undoubtedly, certain finer fibers that enable us to perceive truths when logical deduction, or any other willful effort of the brain, is futile. For a time I wavered, imprest by the professor's authority, but soon became convinced I was right and undertook the task with all the fire and boundless confidence of youth.

I started by first picturing in my mind a direct-current machine, running it and following the changing flow of the currents in the armature. Then I would imagine an alternator and investigate the processes taking place in a similar manner. Next I would visualize systems comprising motors and generators and operate them in various ways. The images I saw were to me perfectly real and tangible. All my remaining term in Gratz was passed in intense but fruitless efforts of this kind, and I almost came to the conclusion that the problem was insolvable.

In 1880 I went to Prague, Bohemia, carrying out my father's wish to complete my education at the University there. It was in that city that I made a decided advance, which consisted in detaching the commutator from the machine and studying the phenomena in this new aspect, but still without result. In the year following there was a sudden change in my views of life. I realized that my parents had been making too great sacrifices on my account and resolved to relieve them of the burden. The wave of the American telephone had just reached the European continent and the system was to be installed in Budapest, Hungary. It appeared an ideal opportunity, all the more as a friend of our family was at the head of the enterprise. It was here that I suffered the complete breakdown of the nerves to which I have referred.

What I experienced during the period of that illness surpasses all belief. My sight and hearing were always extraordinary. I could clearly discern objects in the distance when others saw no trace of them. Several times in my boyhood I saved the houses of our neighbors from fire by hearing the faint crackling sounds which did not disturb their sleep, and calling for help. In 1899, when I was past 40 and carrying on my experiments in Colorado, I could hear very distinctly thunderclaps at a distance of 550 miles. The limit of audition for my young assistants was scarcely more than 150 miles. My ear was thus over 13 times more sensitive. Yet at that time I was, so to speak, stone deaf in comparison with the acuteness of my hearing while under the nervous strain. In Budapest I could hear the ticking of a watch with three rooms between me and the time-piece. A fly alighting on a table in the room would cause a dull thud in my ear. A carriage passing at a distance of a few miles fairly shook my whole body. The whistle of a locomotive 20 or 30 miles away made the bench or chair on which I sat vibrate so strongly that the pain was unbearable. The ground under my feet trembled continuously. I had to support my bed on rubber cushions to get any rest at all. The roaring noises from near and far often produced the effect of spoken words which would have frightened me had I not been able to resolve them into their accidental components. The sun's rays, when periodically intercepted, would cause blows of such force on my brain that they would stun me. I had to summon all my willpower to pass under a bridge or other structure as I experienced a crushing pressure on the skull. In the dark I had the sense of a bat and could detect the presence of an object at a distance of 12 feet by a peculiar creepy sensation on the forehead. My pulse varied from a few to 260 beats and all the tissues of the body quivered with twitches and tremors which was perhaps the hardest to bear. A renowned physician who gave me daily large doses of Bromide of Potassium pronounced my malady unique and incurable.

It is my eternal regret that I was not under the observation of experts in physiology and psychology at that time. I clung desperately to life, but never expected to recover. Can anyone believe that so hopeless a physical wreck could ever be transformed into a man of astonishing strength and tenacity, able to work 38 years almost without a day's interruption, and find himself still strong and fresh in body and mind? Such is my case. A powerful desire to live and to continue the work, and the assistance of a devoted friend and athlete accomplished the wonder. My health returned and with it the vigor of mind. In attacking the problem again I almost regretted that the struggle was soon to end. I had so much energy to spare. When I undertook the task it was not with a resolve such as men often make. With me it was a sacred vow, a question of life and death. I knew that I would perish if I failed. Now I felt that the battle was won. Back in the deep recesses of the brain was the solution, but I could not yet give it outward expression. One afternoon, which is ever present in my recollection, I was enjoying a walk with my friend in the City Park and reciting poetry. At that age I knew entire books by heart, word for word. One of these was Goethe's *Faust*. The sun was just setting and reminded me of the glorious passage:

"Sie rückt und weicht, der Tag ist überlebt,
Dort eilt sie hin und fördert neues Leben.
Oh, daß kein Flügel mich vom Boden hebt
Ihr nach und immer nach zu streben!

Ein schoner Traum indessen sie entweicht,
Ach! zu des Geistes Flügeln wird so leicht
Kein körperlicher Flügel sich gesellen!"

(The glow retreats, done is the day of toil;
It yonder hastes, new fields of life exploring;
Ah, that no wing can lift me from the soil
Upon its track to follow, follow soaring!

A glorious dream! though now the glories fade.
Alas! the wings that lift the mind no aid
Of wings to lift the body can bequeath me.)

As I uttered these inspiring words the idea came like a flash of lightning and in an instant the truth was revealed. I drew with a stick on the sand the diagrams shown six years later in my address before the American Institute of Electrical Engineers, and my companion understood them perfectly. The images I saw were wonderfully sharp and clear and had the solidity of metal and stone, so much so that I told him: "See my motor here; watch me reverse it." I cannot begin to describe my emotions. Pygmalion seeing his statue come to life could not have been more deeply moved. A thousand secrets of nature which I might have stumbled upon accidentally I would have given for that one which I had wrested from her against all odds and at the peril of my existence.

Chapter 4

The Discovery of the Tesla Coil and Transformer

For a while I gave myself up entirely to the intense enjoyment of picturing machines and devising new forms. It was a mental state of happiness about as complete as I have ever known in life. Ideas came in an uninterrupted stream and the only difficulty I had was to hold them fast. The pieces of apparatus I conceived were to me absolutely real and tangible in every detail, even to the minute marks and signs of wear. I delighted in imagining the motors constantly running, for in this way they presented to mind's eye a more fascinating sight. When natural inclination develops into a passionate desire, one advances towards his goal in seven-league boots. In less than two months I evolved virtually all the types of motors and modifications of the system which are now identified with my name. It was, perhaps, providential that the necessities of existence commanded a temporary halt to this consuming activity of the mind. I came to Budapest prompted by a premature report concerning the telephone enterprise and, as irony of fate willed it, I had to accept a position as draftsman in the Central Telegraph Office of the Hungarian Government at a salary which I deem it my privilege not to disclose! Fortunately, I soon won the interest of the Inspector-in-Chief and was thereafter employed on calculations, designs and estimates in connection with new installations, until the Telephone Exchange was started, when I took charge of the same. The knowledge and practical experience I gained in the course of this work was most valuable and the employment gave me ample opportunities for the exercise of my inventive faculties. I made several improvements in the Central Station apparatus and perfected a telephone repeater or amplifier which was never patented or publicly described but would be creditable to me even today. In recognition of my efficient assistance the organizer of the undertaking, Mr. Puskas, upon disposing of his business in Budapest, offered me a position in Paris which I gladly accepted.

I never can forget the deep impression that magic city produced on my mind. For several days after my arrival I roamed through the streets in utter bewilderment of the new spectacle. The attractions were many and irresistible, but, alas, the income was spent as soon as received. When Mr. Puskas asked me how I was getting along in the new sphere, I described the situation accurately in the statement that "the last 29 days of the month are the toughest!" I led a rather strenuous life in what would now be termed "Rooseveltian fashion." Every morning, regardless of weather, I would go from the Boulevard St. Marcel, where I resided, to a bathing house on the Seine, plunge into the water, loop the circuit 27 times and then walk an hour to reach Ivry, where the Company's factory was located. There I would have a woodchopper's breakfast at 7:30 a.m. and then eagerly await the lunch hour, in the meanwhile cracking hard nuts for the Manager of the Works, Mr. Charles Batchellor, who was an intimate friend and assistant of Edison. Here I was thrown in contact with a few Americans who fairly fell in love with me because of my proficiency in billiards. To these men I explained my invention and one of them, Mr. D. Cunningham, Foreman of the Mechanical Department, offered to form a stock company. The proposal seemed to me comical in the extreme. I did not have the faintest conception of what that meant except that it was an American way of doing things. Nothing came of it, however, and during the next few months I had to travel from one to another place in France and Germany to cure the ills of the power plants. On my return to Paris I submitted to one of the administrators of the Company, Mr. Rau, a plan for improving their dynamos and was given an opportunity. My success was complete and the delighted Directors accorded me the privilege of developing automatic regulators which were much desired. Shortly after there was some trouble with the lighting plant which had been installed at the new railroad station in Strassburg, Alsace. The wiring was defective and on the occasion of the opening ceremonies a large part of a wall was blown out through a short-circuit right in the presence of old Emperor William I. The German

Government refused to take the plant and the French Company was facing a serious loss. On account of my knowledge of the German language and past experience, I was entrusted with the difficult task of straightening out matters and early in 1883 I went to Strassburg on that mission.

Some of the incidents in that city have left an indelible record on my memory. By a curious coincidence, a number of men who subsequently achieved fame, lived there about that time. In later life I used to say, "There were bacteria of greatness in that old town. Others caught the disease but I escaped!" The practical work, correspondence, and conferences with officials kept me preoccupied day and night, but, as soon as I was able to manage I undertook the construction of a simple motor in a mechanical shop opposite the railroad station, having brought with me from Paris some material for that purpose. The consummation of the experiment was, however, delayed until the summer of that year when I finally had the satisfaction of seeing rotation effected by alternating currents of different phase, and without sliding contacts or commutator, as I had conceived a year before. It was an exquisite pleasure but not to compare with the delirium of joy following the first revelation.

Among my new friends was the former Mayor of the city, Mr. Bauzin, whom I had already in a measure acquainted with this and other inventions of mine and whose support I endeavored to enlist. He was sincerely devoted to me and put my project before several wealthy persons but, to my mortification, found no response. He wanted to help me in every possible way and the approach of the first of July, 1919, happens to remind me of a form of "assistance" I received from that charming man, which was not financial but none the less appreciated. In 1870, when the Germans invaded the country, Mr. Bauzin had buried a good sized allotment of St. Estephe of 1801 and he came to the conclusion that he knew no worthier person than myself to consume that precious beverage. This, I may say, is one of the unforgettable incidents to which I have referred. My friend urged me to return to Paris as soon as possible and seek support there. This I was anxious to do but my work and negotiations were protracted owing to all sorts of petty obstacles I encountered so that at times the situation seemed hopeless.

Just to give an idea of German thoroughness and "efficiency," I may mention here a rather funny experience. An incandescent lamp of 16 c.p. was to be placed in a hallway and upon selecting the proper location I ordered the workman to run the wires. After working for a while he concluded that the engineer had to be consulted and this was done. The latter made several objections but ultimately agreed that the lamp should be placed two inches from the spot I had assigned, whereupon the work proceeded. Then the engineer became worried and told me that Inspector Averdeck should be notified. That important person called, investigated, debated, and decided that the lamp should be shifted back two inches, which was the place I had marked. It was not long, however, before Averdeck got cold feet himself and advised me that he had informed Ober-Inspector Hieronimus of the matter and that I should await his decision. It was several days before the Ober-Inspector was able to free himself of other pressing duties but at last he arrived and a two hour debate followed, when he decided to move the lamp two inches farther. My hopes that this was the final act were shattered when the Ober-Inspector returned and said to me: "Regierungsrath Funke is so particular that I would not dare to give an order for placing this lamp without his explicit approval." Accordingly arrangements for a visit from that great man were made. We started cleaning up and polishing early in the morning. Everybody brushed up, I put on my gloves and when Funke came with his retinue he was ceremoniously received. After two hours of deliberation he suddenly exclaimed: "I must be going," and pointing to a place on the ceiling, he ordered me to put the lamp there. It was the exact spot which I had originally chosen.

So it went day after day with variations, but I was determined to achieve at whatever cost and in the end my efforts were rewarded. By the spring of 1884 all the differences were adjusted, the plant formally accepted, and I returned to Paris with pleasing anticipations. One of the administrators had promised me a liberal compensation in case I succeeded, as well as a fair consideration of the improvements I had made in their dynamos and I hoped to realize a substantial sum. There were three administrators whom I shall designate as A, B and C for convenience. When I called on A he told me that B had the say. This gentleman thought that only C could decide and the latter was quite sure that A alone had the power to act. After several laps of this circulus vivios it dawned upon me that my reward was a castle in Spain. The utter failure of my attempts to raise capital for development was another disappointment and when Mr. Batchellor pressed me to go to America with a view of redesigning the Edison machines, I determined to try my fortunes in the Land of Golden Promise. But the chance was nearly missed. I liquefied my modest assets, secured accommodations and found myself at the railroad station as the train was pulling out. At that moment I discovered that my money and tickets were gone. What to do was the question. Hercules had plenty of time to deliberate but I had to decide while running alongside the train with opposite feelings surging in my brain like condenser oscillations. Resolve, helped by dexterity, won out in the nick of time and upon passing through the usual experiences, as trivial as unpleasant, I managed to embark for New York with the remnants of my belongings, some poems and articles I had written, and a package of calculations relating to solutions of an unsolvable integral and to my flying machine. During the voyage I sat most of the time at the stern of the ship watching for an opportunity to save somebody from a watery grave, without the slightest thought of danger. Later when I had absorbed some of the practical American sense I shivered at the recollection and marvelled at my former folly.

I wish that I could put in words my first impressions of this country. In the Arabian Tales I read how genii transported people into a land of dreams to live through delightful adventures. My case was just the reverse. The genii had carried me from a world of dreams into one of realities. What I had left was beautiful, artistic and fascinating in every way; what I saw here was machined, rough and unattractive. A burly policeman was twirling his stick which looked to me as big as a log. I approached him politely with the request to direct me. "Six blocks down, then to the left," he said, with murder in his eyes. "Is this America?" I asked myself in painful surprise. "It is a century behind Europe in civilization." When I went abroad in 1889—five years having elapsed since my arrival here—I became convinced that it was more than one hundred years **AHEAD** of Europe and nothing has happened to this day to change my opinion.

The meeting with Edison was a memorable event in my life. I was amazed at this wonderful man who, without early advantages and scientific training, had accomplished so much. I had studied a dozen languages, delved in literature and art, and had spent my best years in libraries reading all sorts of stuff that fell into my hands, from Newton's *Principia* to the novels of Paul de Kock, and felt that most of my life had been squandered. But it did not take long before I recognized that it was the best thing I could have done. Within a few weeks I had won Edison's confidence and it came about in this way.

The S.S. Oregon, the fastest passenger steamer at that time, had both of its lighting machines disabled and its sailing was delayed. As the superstructure had been built after their installation it was impossible to remove them from the hold. The predicament was a serious one and Edison was much annoyed. In the evening I took the necessary instruments with me and went aboard the vessel where I stayed for the night. The dynamos were in bad condition, having several short-circuits and breaks, but with the assistance of the crew I succeeded in putting them in good shape. At 5:00 a.m. when passing along Fifth Avenue on my way to the shop, I met Edison with Batchellor and a few others as they were returning home to retire. "Here is our Parisian running around at night," he said. When I told him that I was coming from the Oregon and had repaired both machines, he looked at me in silence and walked away without another word. But when he had gone some distance I heard him remark: "Batchellor, this is a damn good man." and from that time on I had full freedom in directing the work. For nearly a year my regular hours were from 10:30 a.m. until 5:00 a.m. the next morning without a day's exception. Edison said to me, "I have had many hard-working assistants but you take the cake." During this period I designed 24 different types of standard machines with short cores and of uniform pattern which replaced the old ones. The Manager had promised me $50,000 on the completion of this task but it turned out to be a practical joke. This gave me a painful shock and I resigned my position.

Immediately thereafter some people approached me with the proposal of forming an arc light company under my name, to which I agreed. Here finally was an opportunity to develop the motor, but when I broached the subject to my new associates they said: "No, we want the arc lamp. We don't care for this alternating current of yours." In 1886 my system of arc lighting was perfected and adopted for factory and municipal lighting, and I was free, but with no other possession than a beautifully engraved certificate of stock of hypothetical value. Then followed a period of struggle in the new medium for which I was not fitted, but the reward came in the end and in April, 1887, the Tesla Electric Company was organized, providing a laboratory and facilities. The motors I built there were exactly as I had imagined them. I made no attempt to improve the design, but merely reproduced the pictures as they appeared to my vision and the operation was always as I expected.

In the early part of 1888 an arrangement was made with the Westinghouse Company for the manufacture of the motors on a large scale. But great difficulties had still to be overcome. My system was based on the use of low frequency currents and the Westinghouse experts had adopted 133 cycles with the object of securing advantages in the transformation. They did not want to depart from their standard forms of apparatus and my efforts had to be concentrated upon adapting the motor to these conditions. Another necessity was to produce a motor capable of running efficiently at this frequency on two wires which was not easy to accomplish.

At the close of 1889, however, my services in Pittsburg being no longer essential, I returned to New York and resumed experimental work in a laboratory on Grand Street, where I began immediately the design of high frequency machines. The problems of construction in this unexplored field were novel and quite peculiar and I encountered many difficulties. I rejected the inductor type, fearing that it might not yield perfect sine waves which were so important to resonant action. Had it not been for this I could have saved myself a great deal of labor. Another discouraging feature of the high frequency alternator seemed to be the inconstancy of speed which threatened to impose serious limitations to its use. I had already noted in my demonstrations before the American Institution of Electrical Engineers that several times the tune was lost, necessitating readjustment, and did not yet foresee, what I discovered long afterwards, a means of operating a machine of this kind at a speed constant to such a degree as not to vary more than a small fraction of one revolution between the extremes of load.

From many other considerations it appeared desirable to invent a simpler device for the production of electric oscillations. In 1856 Lord Kelvin had exposed the theory of the condenser discharge, but no practical application of that important knowledge was made. I saw the possibilities and undertook the development of induction apparatus on this principle. My progress was so rapid as to enable me to exhibit at my lecture in 1891 a coil giving sparks of five inches. On that occasion I frankly told the engineers of a defect involved in the transformation by the new method, namely, the loss in the spark gap. Subsequent investigation showed that no matter what medium is employed, be it air, hydrogen, mercury vapor, oil or a stream of electrons, the efficiency is the same. It is a law very much like that governing the conversion of mechanical energy. We may drop a weight from a certain height vertically down or carry it to the lower level along any devious path, it is immaterial insofar as the amount of work is concerned. Fortunately however, this drawback is not fatal as by proper proportioning of the resonant circuits an efficiency of 85% is attainable. Since my early announcement of the invention it has come into universal use and wrought a revolution in many departments. But a still greater future awaits it. When in 1900 I obtained powerful discharges of 100 feet and flashed a current around the globe, I was reminded of the first tiny spark I observed in my Grand Street laboratory and was thrilled by sensations akin to those I felt when I discovered the rotating magnetic field.

Chapter 5

The Magnifying Transmitter

As I review the events of my past life I realize how subtle are the influences that shape our destinies. An incident of my youth may serve to illustrate. One winter's day I managed to climb a steep mountain, in company with other boys. The snow was quite deep and a warm southerly wind made it just suitable for our purpose. We amused ourselves by throwing balls which would roll down a certain distance, gathering more or less snow, and we tried to outdo one another in this exciting sport. Suddenly a ball was seen to go beyond the limit, swelling to enormous proportions until it became as big as a house and plunged thundering into the valley below with a force that made the ground tremble. I looked on spellbound, incapable of understanding what had happened. For weeks afterwards the picture of the avalanche was before my eyes and I wondered how anything so small could grow to such an immense size. Ever since that time the magnification of feeble actions fascinated me, and when, years later, I took up the experimental study of mechanical and electrical resonance, I was keenly interested from the very start. Possibly, had it not been for that early powerful impression, I might not have followed up the little spark I obtained with my coil and never developed my best invention, the true history of which I'll tell here for the first time.

"Lionhunters" have often asked me which of my discoveries I prize most. This depends on the point of view. Not a few technical men, very able in their special departments, but dominated by a pedantic spirit and near-sighted, have asserted that excepting the induction motor I have given to the world little of practical use. This is a grievous mistake. A new idea must not be judged by its immediate results. My alternating system of power transmission came at a psychological moment, as a long-sought answer to pressing industrial questions, and although considerable resistance had to be overcome and opposing interests reconciled, as usual, the commercial introduction could not be long delayed. Now, compare this situation with that confronting my turbine, for example. One should think that so simple and beautiful an invention, possessing many features of an ideal motor, should be adopted at once and, undoubtedly, it would under similar conditions. But the prospective effect of the rotating field was not to render worthless existing machinery; on the contrary, it was to give it additional value. The system lent itself to new enterprise as well as to improvement of the old. My turbine is an advance of a character entirely different. It is a radical departure in the sense that its success would mean the abandonment of the antiquated types of prime movers on which billions of dollars have been spent. Under such circumstances the progress must be slow and perhaps the greatest impediment is encountered in the prejudicial opinions created in the minds of experts by organized opposition.

Only the other day I had a disheartening experience when I met my friend and former assistant, Charles F. Scott, now Professor of Electrical Engineering at Yale. I had not seen him for a long time and was glad to have an opportunity for a little chat at my office. Our conversation naturally enough drifted on my turbine and I became heated to a high degree. "Scott," I exclaimed, carried away by the vision of a glorious future, "my turbine will scrap all the heat-engines in the world." Scott stroked his chin and looked away thoughtfully, as though making a mental calculation. "That will make quite a pile of scrap," he said, and left without another word!

These and other inventions of mine, however, were nothing more than steps forward in certain directions. In evolving them I simply followed the inborn sense to improve the present devices without any special thought of our far more imperative necessities. The "Magnifying Transmitter" was the product of labors extending through years, having for their chief object the solution of problems which are infinitely more important to mankind than mere industrial development.

If my memory serves me right, it was in November, 1890, that I performed a laboratory experiment which was one of the most extraordinary and spectacular ever recorded in the annals of science. In investigating the behaviour of high frequency currents I had satisfied myself that an electric field of sufficient intensity could be produced in a room to light up electrodeless vacuum tubes. Accordingly, a transformer was built to test the theory and the first trial proved a marvelous success. It is difficult to appreciate what those strange phenomena meant at that time. We crave for new sensations but soon become indifferent to them. The wonders of yesterday are today common occurrences. When my tubes were first publicly exhibited they were viewed with amazement impossible to describe. From all parts of the world I received urgent invitations and numerous honors and other flattering inducements were offered to me, which I declined.

But in 1892 the demands became irresistible and I went to London where I delivered a lecture before the Institution of Electrical Engineers. It had been my intention to leave immediately for Paris in compliance with a similar obligation, but Sir James Dewar insisted on my appearing before the Royal Institution. I was a man of firm resolve but succumbed easily to the forceful arguments of the great Scotsman. He pushed me into a chair and poured out half a glass of a wonderful brown fluid which sparkled in all sorts of iridescent colors and tasted like nectar. "Now," said he, "you are sitting in Faraday's chair and you are enjoying whiskey he used to drink." In both aspects it was an enviable experience. The next evening I gave a demonstration before that

Institution, at the termination of which Lord Rayleigh addressed the audience and his generous words gave me the first start in these endeavors. I fled from London and later from Paris to escape favors showered upon me, and journeyed to my home where I passed through a most painful ordeal and illness. Upon regaining my health I began to formulate plans for the resumption of work in America. Up to that time I never realized that I possessed any particular gift of discovery but Lord Rayleigh, whom I always considered as an ideal man of science, had said so and if that was the case I felt that I should concentrate on some big idea.

One day, as I was roaming in the mountains, I sought shelter from an approaching storm. The sky became overhung with heavy clouds but somehow the rain was delayed until, all of a sudden, there was a lightning flash and a few moments after a deluge. This observation set me thinking. It was manifest that the two phenomena were closely related, as cause and effect, and a little reflection led me to the conclusion that the electrical energy involved in the precipitation of the water was inconsiderable, the function of lightning being much like that of a sensitive trigger.

Here was a stupendous possibility of achievement. If we could produce electric effects of the required quality, this whole planet and the conditions of existence on it could be transformed. The sun raises the water of the oceans and winds drive it to distant regions where it remains in a state of most delicate balance. If it were in our power to upset it when and wherever desired, this mighty life-sustaining stream could be at will controlled. We could irrigate arid deserts, create lakes and rivers and provide motive power in unlimited amounts. This would be the most efficient way of harnessing the sun to the uses of man. The consummation depended on our ability to develop electric forces of the order of those in nature. It seemed a hopeless undertaking, but I made up my mind to try it and immediately on my return to the United States, in the Summer of 1892, work was begun which was to me all the more attractive, because a means of the same kind was necessary for the successful transmission of energy without wires.

The first gratifying result was obtained in the spring of the succeeding year when I reached tensions of about 1,000,000 volts with my conical coil. That was not much in the light of the present art, but it was then considered a feat. Steady progress was made until the destruction of my laboratory by fire in 1895, as may be judged from an article by T. C. Martin which appeared in the April number of the *Century Magazine*. This calamity set me back in many ways and most of that year had to be devoted to planning and reconstruction. However, as soon as circumstances permitted, I returned to the task.

Although I knew that higher electro-motive forces were attainable with apparatus of larger dimensions, I had an instinctive perception that the object could be accomplished by the proper design of a comparatively small and compact transformer. In carrying on tests with a secondary in the form of a flat spiral, as illustrated in my patents, the absence of streamers surprised me, and it was not long before I discovered that this was due to the position of the turns and their mutual action. Profiting from this observation I resorted to the use of a high tension conductor with turns of considerable diameter sufficiently separated to keep down the distributed capacity, while at the same time preventing undue accumulation of the charge at any point. The application of this principle enabled me to produce pressures of 4,000,000 volts, which was about the limit obtainable in my new laboratory at Houston Street, as the discharges extended through a distance of 16 feet. A photograph of this transmitter was published in the *Electrical Review* of November, 1898.

In order to advance further along this line I had to go into the open, and in the spring of 1899, having completed preparations for the erection of a wireless plant, I went to Colorado where I remained for more than one year. Here I introduced other improvements and refinements which made it possible to generate currents of any tension that may be desired. Those who are interested will find some information in regard to the experiments I conducted there in my article, "The Problem of Increasing Human Energy" in the *Century Magazine* of June, 1900, to which I have referred on a previous occasion.

I have been asked by the *Electrical Experimenter* to be quite explicit on this subject so that my young friends among the readers of the magazine will clearly understand the construction and operation of my "Magnifying

Transmitter" and the purposes for which it is intended. Well, then, in the first place, it is a resonant transformer with a secondary in which the parts, charged to a high potential, are of considerable area and arranged in space along ideal enveloping surfaces of very large radii of curvature, and at proper distances from one another thereby insuring a small electric surface density everywhere so that no leak can occur even if the conductor is bare. It is suitable for any frequency, from a few to many thousands of cycles per second, and can be used in the production of currents of tremendous volume and moderate pressure, or of smaller amperage and immense electromotive force. The maximum electric tension is merely dependent on the curvature of the surfaces on which the charged elements are situated and the area of the latter.

Judging from my past experience, as much as 100,000,000 volts are perfectly practicable. On the other hand currents of many thousands of amperes may be obtained in the antenna. A plant of but very moderate dimensions is required for such performances. Theoretically, a terminal of less than 90 feet in diameter is sufficient to develop an electromotive force of that magnitude while for antenna currents of from 2,000 to 4,000 amperes at the usual frequencies it need not be larger than 30 feet in diameter.

In a more restricted meaning this wireless transmitter is one in which the Hertz-wave radiation is an entirely negligible quantity as compared with the whole energy, under which condition the damping factor is extremely small and an enormous charge is stored in the elevated capacity. Such a circuit may then be excited with impulses of any kind, even of low frequency and it will yield sinusoidal and continuous oscillations like those of an alternator.

Taken in the narrowest significance of the term, however, it is a resonant transformer which, besides possessing these qualities, is accurately proportioned to fit the globe and its electrical constants and properties, by virtue of which design it becomes highly efficient and effective in the wireless transmission of energy. Distance is then absolutely eliminated, there being no diminution in the intensity of the transmitted impulses. It is even possible to make the actions increase with the distance from the plant according to an exact mathematical law.

This invention was one of a number comprised in my "World-System" of wireless transmission which I undertook to commercialize on my return to New York in 1900. As to the immediate purposes of my enterprise, they were clearly outlined in a technical statement of that period from which I quote, "The 'World-System' has resulted from a combination of several original discoveries made by the inventor in the course of long continued research and experimentation. It makes possible not only the instantaneous and precise wireless transmission of any kind of signals, messages or characters, to all parts of the world, but also the inter-connection of the existing telegraph, telephone, and other signal stations without any change in their present equipment. By its means, for instance, a telephone subscriber here may call up and talk to any other subscriber on the globe. An inexpensive receiver, not bigger than a watch, will enable him to listen anywhere, on land or sea, to a speech delivered or music played in some other place, however distant. These examples are cited merely to give an idea of the possibilities of this great scientific advance, which annihilates distance and makes that perfect natural conductor, the Earth, available for all the innumerable purposes which human ingenuity has found for a line-wire. One far-reaching result of this is that any device capable of being operated through one or more wires (at a distance obviously restricted) can likewise be actuated, without artificial conductors and with the same facility and accuracy, at distances to which there are no limits other than those imposed by the physical dimensions of the globe. Thus, not only will entirely new fields for commercial exploitation be opened up by this ideal method of transmission but the old ones vastly extended. The 'World-System' is based on the application of the following important inventions and discoveries:

1. The 'Tesla Transformer.' This apparatus is in the production of electrical vibrations as revolutionary as gunpowder was in warfare. Currents many times stronger than any ever generated in the usual ways, and sparks over 100 feet long, have been produced by the inventor with an instrument of this kind.

2. The 'Magnifying Transmitter.' This is Tesla's best invention, a peculiar transformer specially adapted to excite the Earth, which is in the transmission of electrical energy what the telescope is in astronomical observation. By the use of this marvelous device he has already set up electrical movements of greater intensity than those of lightning and passed a current, sufficient to light more than two hundred incandescent lamps, around the globe.
3. The 'Tesla Wireless System.' This system comprises a number of improvements and is the only means known for transmitting economically electrical energy to a distance without wires. Careful tests and measurements in connection with an experimental station of great activity, erected by the inventor in Colorado, have demonstrated that power in any desired amount can be conveyed, clear across the globe if necessary, with a loss not exceeding a few percent.
4. The 'Art of Individualization.' This invention of Tesla's is to primitive 'tuning' what refined language is to unarticulated expression. It makes possible the transmission of signals or messages absolutely secret and exclusive both in the active and passive aspect, that is, non-interfering as well as secure. Each signal is like an individual of unmistakable identity and there is virtually no limit to the number of stations

or instruments which can be simultaneously operated without the slightest mutual disturbance.

5. 'The Terrestrial Stationary Waves.' This wonderful discovery, popularly explained, means that the Earth is responsive to electrical vibrations of definite pitch just as a tuning fork to certain waves of sound. These particular electrical vibrations, capable of powerfully exciting the globe, lend themselves to innumerable uses of great importance commercially and in many other respects.

The first 'World-System' power plant can be put in operation in nine months. With this power plant it will be practicable to attain electrical activities up to ten million horsepower and it is designed to serve for as many technical achievements as are possible without due expense. Among these the following may be mentioned:

1. The inter-connection of the existing telegraph exchanges or offices all over the world;
2. The establishment of a secret and secure government telegraph service;
3. The inter-connection of all the present telephone exchanges or offices on the globe;
4. The universal distribution of general news, by telegraph or telephone, in connection with the press;

5. The establishment of such a 'World-System' of intelligence transmission for exclusive private use;
6. The inter-connection and operation of all stock tickers of the world;
7. The establishment of a 'World-System' of musical distribution, etc.;
8. The universal registration of time by cheap clocks indicating the hour with astronomical precision and requiring no attention whatever;
9. The world transmission of typed or hand-written characters, letters, checks, etc.;
10. The establishment of a universal marine service enabling the navigators of all ships to steer perfectly without compass, to determine the exact location, hour and speed, to prevent collisions and disasters, etc.;
11. The inauguration of a system of world-printing on land and sea;
12. The world reproduction of photographic pictures and all kinds of drawings or records."

I also proposed to make demonstrations in the wireless transmission of power on a small scale but sufficient to carry conviction. Besides these I referred to other and incomparably more important applications of my discoveries which will be disclosed at some future date.

A plant was built on Long Island with a tower 187 feet high, having a spherical terminal about 68 feet in diameter. These dimensions were adequate for the transmission of virtually any amount of energy. Originally only from 200 to 300 kW were provided but I intended to employ later several thousand horsepower. The transmitter was to emit a wave complex of special characteristics and I had devised a unique method of telephonic control of any amount of energy.

The tower was destroyed two years ago but my projects are being developed and another one, improved in some features, will be constructed. On this occasion I would contradict the widely circulated report that the structure was demolished by the Government which owing to war conditions, might have created prejudice in the minds of those who may not know that the papers, which 30 years ago conferred upon me the honor of American citizenship, are always kept in a safe, while my orders, diplomas, degrees, gold medals and other distinctions are packed away in old trunks. If this report had a foundation I would have been refunded a large sum of money which I expended in the construction of the tower. On the contrary it was in the interest of the Government to preserve it, particularly as it would have made possible—to mention just one valuable result—the location of a submarine in any part of the world. My plant, services, and all my improvements have always been at the disposal of the officials and ever since the outbreak of the European conflict I have been working at a sacrifice on several inventions of mine relating to aerial navigation, ship propulsion and wireless transmission which are of the greatest importance to the country.

Those who are well informed know that my ideas have revolutionized the industries of the United States and I am not aware that there lives an inventor who has been, in this respect, as fortunate as myself especially as regards the use of his improvements in the war. I have refrained from publicly expressing myself on this subject before as it seemed improper to dwell on personal matters while all the world was in dire trouble.

I would add further, in view of various rumors which have reached me, that Mr. J. Pierpont Morgan did not interest himself with me in a business way but in the same large spirit in which he has assisted many other pioneers. He carried out his generous promise to the letter and it would have been most unreasonable to expect from him anything more. He had the highest regard for my attainments and gave me every evidence of his complete faith in my ability to ultimately achieve what I had set out to do. I am unwilling to accord to some small-minded and jealous individuals the satisfaction of having thwarted my efforts. These men are to me nothing more than microbes of a nasty disease. My project was retarded by laws of nature. The world was not prepared for it. It was too far ahead of time. But the same laws will prevail in the end and make it a triumphal success.

Chapter 6
The Art of Telautomatics

No subject to which I have ever devoted myself has called for such concentration of mind and strained to so dangerous a degree the finest fibers of my brain as the system of which the Magnifying Transmitter is the foundation. I put all the intensity and vigor of youth in the development of the rotating field discoveries, but those early labors were of a different character. Although strenuous in the extreme, they did not involve that keen and exhausting discernment which had to be exercised in attacking the many puzzling problems of the wireless. Despite my rare physical endurance at that period the abused nerves finally rebelled and I suffered a complete collapse, just as the consummation of the long and difficult task was almost in sight.

Without doubt I would have paid a greater penalty later, and very likely my career would have been prematurely terminated, had not providence equipped me with a safety device, which has seemed to improve with advancing years and unfailingly comes into play when my forces are at an end. So long as it operates I am safe from danger, due to overwork, which threatens other inventors and, incidentally, I need no vacations which are indispensable to most people. When I am all but used up I simply do as the darkies, who "naturally fall asleep while white folks worry." To venture a theory out of my sphere, the body probably accumulates little by little a definite quantity of some toxic agent and I sink into a nearly lethargic state which lasts half an hour to the minute. Upon awakening I have the sensation as though the events immediately preceding had occurred very long ago, and if I attempt to continue the interrupted train of thought I feel a veritable mental nausea. Involuntarily I then turn to other work and am surprised at the freshness of the mind and ease with which I overcome obstacles that had baffled me before. After weeks or months my passion for the temporarily abandoned invention returns and I invariably find answers to all the vexing questions with scarcely any effort.

In this connection I will tell of an extraordinary experience which may be of interest to students of psychology. I had produced a striking phenomenon with my grounded transmitter and was endeavoring to ascertain its true significance in relation to the currents propagated through the earth. It seemed a hopeless undertaking, and for more than a year I worked unremittingly, but in vain. This profound study so entirely absorbed me that I became forgetful of everything else, even of my undermined health. At last, as I was at the point of breaking down, nature applied the preservative inducing lethal sleep. Regaining my senses I realized with consternation that I was unable to visualize scenes from my life except those of infancy, the very first ones that had entered my consciousness. Curiously enough, these appeared before my vision with startling distinctness and afforded me welcome relief. Night after night, when retiring, I would think of them and more and more of my previous existence was revealed. The image of my mother was always the principal figure in the spectacle that slowly unfolded, and a consuming desire to see her again gradually took possession of me. This feeling grew so strong that I resolved to drop all work and satisfy my longing. But I found it too hard to break away from the laboratory, and several months elapsed during which I had succeeded in reviving all the impressions of my past life up to the spring of 1892. In the next picture that came out of the mist of oblivion, I saw myself at the Hotel de la Paix in Paris just coming to from one of my peculiar sleeping spells, which had been caused by prolonged exertion of the brain. Imagine the pain and distress I felt when it flashed upon my mind that a dispatch was handed to me at that very moment bearing the sad news that my mother was dying. I remembered how I made the long journey home without an hour of rest and how she passed away after weeks of agony! It was especially remarkable that during all this period of partially obliterated memory I was fully alive to everything touching on the subject of my research. I could recall the smallest details and the least significant observations in my experiments and even recite pages of text and complex mathematical formulae.

My belief is firm in a law of compensation. The true rewards are ever in proportion to the labor and sacrifices made. This is one of the reasons why I feel certain that of all my inventions, the Magnifying Transmitter will prove most important and valuable to future generations. I am prompted to this prediction not so much by thoughts of the commercial and industrial revolution which it will surely bring about, but of the humanitarian consequences of the many achievements it makes possible. Considerations of mere utility weigh little in the balance against the higher benefits of civilization. We are confronted with portentous problems which can not be solved just by providing for our material existence, however abundantly. On the contrary, progress in this direction is fraught with hazards and perils not less menacing than those born from want and suffering. If we were to release the energy of atoms or discover some other way of developing cheap and unlimited power at any point of the globe this accomplishment, instead of being a blessing, might bring disaster to mankind in giving rise to dissension and anarchy which would ultimately result in the enthronement of the hated regime of force. The greatest good will comes from technical improvements tending to unification and harmony, and my wireless transmitter is preeminently such. By its means the human voice and likeness will be reproduced everywhere and factories driven thousands of miles from waterfalls furnishing the power; aerial machines will be propelled around the earth without a stop and the sun's energy controlled to create lakes and rivers for motive purposes and transformation of arid deserts into fertile land. Its introduction for telegraphic, telephonic and similar uses will automatically cut out the statics and all other interferences which at present impose narrow limits to the application of the wireless.

This is a timely topic on which a few words might not be amiss.

During the past decade a number of people have arrogantly claimed that they had succeeded in doing away with this impediment. I have carefully examined all of the arrangements described and tested most of them long before they were publicly disclosed, but the finding was uniformly negative. A recent official statement from the U.S. Navy may, perhaps, have taught some beguilable news editors how to appraise these announcements at their real worth. As a rule the attempts are based on theories so fallacious that whenever they come to my notice I can not help thinking in a lighter vein. Quite recently a new discovery was heralded, with a deafening flourish of trumpets, but it proved another case of a mountain bringing forth a mouse.

This reminds me of an exciting incident which took place years ago when I was conducting my experiments with currents of high frequency. Steve Brodie had just jumped off the Brooklyn Bridge. The feat has been vulgarized since by imitators, but the first report electrified New York. I was very impressionable then and frequently spoke of the daring printer. On a hot afternoon I felt the necessity of refreshing myself and stepped into one of the popular thirty thousand institutions of this great city where a delicious 12% beverage was served which can now be had only by making a trip to the poor and devastated countries of Europe. The attendance was large and not over-distinguished and a matter was discussed which gave me an admirable opening for the careless remark: "This is what I said when I jumped off the bridge." No sooner had I uttered these words than I felt like the companion of Timotheus in the poem of Schiller. In an instant there was a pandemonium and a dozen voices cried: "It is Brodie! " I threw a quarter on the counter and bolted for the door but the crowd was at my heels with yells: "Stop, Steve!" which must have been misunderstood for many persons tried to hold me up as I ran frantically for my haven of refuge. By darting around corners I fortunately managed—through the medium of a fire escape—to reach the laboratory where I threw off my coat, camouflaged myself as a hard-working blacksmith, and started the forge. But these precautions proved unnecessary; I had eluded my pursuers. For many years afterwards, at night, when imagination turns into spectres the trifling troubles of the day, I often thought, as I tossed on the bed, what my fate would have been had that mob caught me and found out that I was not Steve Brodie!

Now the engineer, who lately gave an account before a technical body of a novel remedy against statics based on a "heretofore unknown law of nature," seems to have been as reckless as myself when he contended that these disturbances propagate up and down, while those of a transmitter proceed along the earth. It would mean that a condenser, as this globe, with its gaseous envelope, could be charged and discharged in a manner quite contrary to the fundamental teachings propounded in every elemental text-book of physics. Such a supposition would have been condemned as erroneous, even in Franklin's time, for the facts bearing on this were then well known and the identity between atmospheric electricity and that developed by machines was fully established. Obviously, natural and artificial disturbances propagate through the earth and the air in exactly the same way, and both set up electromotive forces in the horizontal, as well as vertical, sense. Interference can not be overcome by any such methods as were proposed. The truth is this: in the air the potential increases at the rate of about 50 volts per foot of elevation, owing to which there may be a difference of pressure amounting to 20, or even 40,000 volts between the upper and lower ends of the antenna. The masses of the charged atmosphere are constantly in motion and give up electricity to the conductor, not continuously but rather disruptively, this producing a grinding noise in a sensitive telephonic receiver. The higher the terminal and the greater the space encompassed by the wires, the more pronounced is the effect, but it must be understood that it is purely local and has little to do with the real trouble.

In 1900, while perfecting my wireless system, one form of apparatus comprised four antennae. These were carefully calibrated to the same frequency and connected in multiple with the object of magnifying the action, in receiving from any direction. When I desired to ascertain the origin of the transmitted impulses, each diagonally situated pair was put in series with a primary coil energizing the detector circuit. In the former case the sound was loud in the telephone; in the latter it ceased, as expected, the two antennae neutralizing each other, but the true statics manifested themselves in both instances and I had to devise special preventives embodying different principles.

By employing receivers connected to two points of the ground, as suggested by me long ago, this trouble caused by the charged air, which is very serious in the structures as now built, is nullified and besides, the liability of all kinds of interference is reduced to about one-half, because of the directional character of the circuit. This was perfectly self-evident, but came as a revelation to some simple-minded wireless folks whose experience was confined to forms of apparatus that could have been improved with an axe, and they have been disposing of the bear's skin before killing him. If it were true that strays performed such antics, it would be easy to get rid of them by receiving without aerials. But, as a matter of fact, a wire buried in the ground which, conforming to this view, should be absolutely immune, is more susceptible to certain extraneous impulses than one placed vertically in the air. To state it fairly, a slight progress has been made, but not by virtue of any particular method or device. It was achieved simply by discarding the enormous structures, which are bad enough for transmission but wholly unsuitable for reception, and adopting a more appropriate type of receiver. As I pointed out in a previous article, to dispose of this difficulty for good, a radical change must be made in the system, and the sooner this is done the better.

It would be calamitous, indeed, if at this time when the art is in its infancy and the vast majority, not excepting even experts, have no conception of its ultimate possibilities, a measure would be rushed through the legislature making it a government monopoly. This was proposed a few weeks ago by Secretary Daniels, and no doubt that distinguished official has made his appeal to the Senate and House of Representatives with sincere conviction. But universal evidence unmistakably shows that the best results are always obtained in healthful commercial competition. There are, however, exceptional reasons why wireless should be given the fullest freedom of development. In the first place it offers prospects immeasurably greater and more vital to betterment of human life than any other invention or discovery in the history of man. Then again, it must be understood that this wonderful art has been, in its entirety, evolved here and can be called "American" with more right and propriety than the telephone, the incandescent lamp or the aeroplane. Enterprising press agents and stock jobbers have been so successful in spreading misinformation that even so excellent a periodical as the *Scientific American* accords the chief credit to a foreign country. The Germans, of course, gave us the Hertz-waves and the Russian, English, French and Italian experts were quick in using them for signaling purposes. It was an obvious application of the new agent and accomplished with the old classical and unimproved induction coil—scarcely anything more than another kind of heliography. The radius of transmission was very limited, the results attained of little value, and the Hertz oscillations, as a means for conveying intelligence, could have been advantageously replaced by sound-waves, which I advocated in 1891. Moreover, all of these attempts were made three years after the basic principles of the wireless system, which is universally employed today, and its potent instrumentalities had been clearly described and developed in America. No trace of those Hertzian appliances and methods remains today. We have proceeded in the very opposite direction and what has been done is the product of the brains and efforts of citizens of this country. The fundamental patents have expired and the opportunities are open to all. The chief argument of the Secretary is based on interference. According to his statement, reported in the *New York Herald* of July 29th, signals from a powerful station can be intercepted in every village of the world. In view of this fact, which was demonstrated in my experiments of 1900, it would be of little use to impose restrictions in the United States.

As throwing light on this point, I may mention that only recently an odd looking gentleman called on me with the object of enlisting my services in the construction of world transmitters in some distant land. "We have no money," he said, "but carloads of solid gold and we will give you a liberal amount." I told him that I wanted to see first what will be done with my inventions in America, and this ended the interview. But I am satisfied that some dark forces are at work, and as time goes on the maintenance of continuous communication will be rendered more difficult. The only remedy is a system immune against interruption. It has been perfected, it exists, and all that is necessary is to put it in operation.

The terrible conflict is still uppermost in the minds and perhaps the greatest importance will be attached to the Magnifying Transmitter as a machine for attack and defense, more particularly in connection with Telautomatics. This invention is a logical outcome of observations begun in my boyhood and continued throughout my life. When the first results were published the *Electrical Review* stated editorially that it would become one of the "most potent factors in the advance and civilization of mankind." The time is not distant when this prediction will be fulfilled. In 1898 and 1900 it was offered to the Government and might have been adopted were I one of those who would go to Alexander's shepherd when they want a favor from Alexander. At that time I really thought that it would abolish war, because of its unlimited destructiveness and exclusion of the personal element of combat. But while I have not lost faith in its potentialities, my views have changed since.

War can not be avoided until the physical cause for its recurrence is removed and this, in the last analysis, is the vast extent of the planet on which we live. Only through annihilation of distance in every respect, as the conveyance of intelligence, transport of passengers and supplies and transmission of energy will conditions be brought about some day, insuring permanency of friendly relations. What we now want most is closer contact and better understanding between individuals and communities all over the earth, and the elimination of that fanatic devotion to exalted ideals of national egoism and pride which is always prone to plunge the world into primeval barbarism and strife. No league or parliamentary act of any kind will ever prevent such a calamity. These are only new devices for putting the weak at the mercy of the strong. I have expressed myself in this regard 14 years ago, when a combination of a few leading governments—a sort of Holy Alliance—was advocated by the late Andrew Carnegie, who may be fairly considered as the father of this idea, having given to it more publicity and impetus than anybody else prior to the efforts of the President. While it can not be denied that such a pact might be of material advantage to some less fortunate peoples, it can not attain the chief object sought. Peace can only come as a natural consequence of universal enlightenment and merging of races, and we are still far from this blissful realization.

As I view the world of today, in the light of the gigantic struggle we have witnessed, I am filled with conviction that the interests of humanity would be best served if the United States remained true to its traditions and kept out of "entangling alliances." Situated as it is, geographically, remote from the theaters of impending conflicts, without incentive to territorial aggrandizement, with inexhaustible resources and immense population thoroughly imbued with the spirit of liberty and right, this country is placed in a unique and privileged position. It is thus able to exert, independently, its colossal strength and moral force to the benefit of all, more judiciously and effectively, than as member of a league.

In one of these biographical sketches, published in the *Electrical Experimenter*, I have dwelt on the circumstances of my early life and told of an affliction which compelled me to unremitting exercise of imagination and self observation. This mental activity, at first involuntary under the pressure of illness and suffering, gradually became second nature and led me finally to recognize that I was but an automaton devoid of free will in thought and action and merely responsive to the forces of the environment. Our bodies are of such complexity of structure, the motions we perform are so numerous and involved, and the external impressions on our sense organs to such a degree delicate and elusive that it is hard for the average person to grasp this fact. And yet nothing is more convincing to the trained investigator than the mechanistic theory of life which had been, in a measure, understood and propounded by Descartes 300 years ago. But in his time many important functions of our organism were unknown and, especially with respect to the nature of light and the construction and operation of the eye, philosophers were in the dark.

In recent years the progress of scientific research in these fields has been such as to leave no room for a doubt in regard to this view on which many works have been published. One of its ablest and most eloquent exponents is, perhaps, Felix Le Dantec, formerly assistant of Pasteur. Prof. Jacques Loeb has performed remarkable experiments in heliotropism, clearly establishing the controlling power of light in lower forms of organisms, and his latest book, *Forced Movements*, is revelatory. But while men of science accept this theory simply as any other that is recognized, to me it is a truth which I hourly demonstrate by every act and thought of mine. The consciousness of the external impression prompting me to any kind of exertion, physical or mental, is ever present in my mind. Only on very rare occasions, when I was in a state of exceptional concentration, have I found difficulty in locating the original impulses.

The by far greater number of human beings are never aware of what is passing around and within them, and millions fall victims of disease and die prematurely just on this account. The most common every-day occurrences appear to them mysterious and inexplicable. One may feel a sudden wave of sadness and rake his brain for an explanation when he might have noticed that it was caused by a cloud cutting off the rays of the sun. He may see the image of a friend dear to him under conditions which he construes as very peculiar, when only shortly before he has passed him in the street or seen his photograph somewhere. When he loses a collar button he fusses and swears for an hour, being unable to visualize his previous actions and locate the object directly. Deficient observation is merely a form of ignorance and responsible for the many morbid notions and foolish ideas prevailing. There is not more than one out of every ten persons who does not believe in telepathy and other psychic manifestations, spiritualism and communion with the dead, and who would refuse to listen to willing or unwilling deceivers.

Just to illustrate how deeply rooted this tendency has become even among the clear-headed American population, I may mention a comical incident.

Shortly before the war, when the exhibition of my turbines in this city elicited widespread comment in the technical papers, I anticipated that there would be a scramble among manufacturers to get hold of the invention, and I had particular designs on that man from Detroit who has an uncanny faculty for accumulating millions. So confident was I that he would turn up some day, that I declared this as certain to my secretary and assistants. Sure enough, one fine morning a body of engineers from the Ford Motor Company presented themselves with the request of discussing with me an important project. "Didn't I tell you?" I remarked triumphantly to my employees, and one of them said, "You are amazing, Mr. Tesla; everything comes out exactly as you predict." As soon as these hard-headed men were seated I, of course, immediately began to extol the wonderful features of my turbine, when the spokesmen interrupted me and said, "We know all about this, but we are on a special errand. We have formed a psychological society for the investigation of psychic phenomena and we want you to join us in this undertaking." I suppose those engineers never knew how near they came to being fired out of my office.

Ever since I was told by some of the greatest men of the time, leaders in science whose names are immortal, that I possess an unusual mind, I bent all my thinking faculties on the solution of great problems regardless of sacrifice. For many years I endeavored to solve the enigma of death, and watched eagerly for every kind of spiritual indication. But only once in the course of my existence have I had an experience which momentarily impressed me as supernatural. It was at the time of my mother's death. I had become completely exhausted by pain and long vigilance, and one night was carried to a building about two blocks from our home. As I lay helpless there, I thought that if my mother died while I was away from her bedside she would surely give me a sign. Two or three months before I was in London in company with my late friend, Sir William Crookes, when spiritualism was discussed, and I was under the full sway of these thoughts. I might not have paid attention to other men, but was susceptible to his arguments as it was his epochal work on radiant matter, which I had read as a student, that made me embrace the electrical career. I reflected that the conditions for a look into the beyond were most favorable, for my mother was a woman of genius and particularly excelling in the powers of intuition. During the whole night every fiber in my brain was strained in expectancy, but nothing happened until early in the morning, when I fell in a sleep, or perhaps a swoon, and saw a cloud carrying angelic figures of marvelous beauty, one of whom gazed upon me lovingly and gradually assumed the features of my mother. The appearance slowly floated across the room and vanished, and I was awakened by an indescribably sweet song of many voices. In that instant a certitude, which no words can express, came upon me that my mother had just died. And that was true. I was unable to understand the tremendous weight of the painful knowledge I received in advance, and wrote a letter to Sir William Crookes while still under the domination of these impressions and in poor bodily health. When I recovered I sought for a long time the external cause of this strange manifestation and, to my great relief, I succeeded after many months of fruitless effort. I had seen the painting of a celebrated artist, representing allegorically one of the seasons in the form of a cloud with a group of angels which seemed to actually float in the air, and this had struck me forcefully. It was exactly the same that appeared in my dream, with the exception of my mother's likeness. The music came from the choir in the church nearby at the early mass of Easter morning, explaining everything satisfactorily in conformity with scientific facts.

This occurred long ago, and I have never had the faintest reason since to change my views on psychical and spiritual phenomena, for which there is absolutely no foundation. The belief in these is the natural outgrowth of intellectual development. Religious dogmas are no longer accepted in their orthodox meaning, but every individual clings to faith in a supreme power of some kind. We all must have an ideal to govern our conduct and insure contentment, but it is immaterial whether it be one of creed, art, science or anything else, so long as it fulfills the function of a dematerializing force. It is essential to the peaceful existence of humanity as a whole that one common conception should prevail.

While I have failed to obtain any evidence in support of the contentions of psychologists and spiritualists, I have proved to my complete satisfaction the automatism of life, not only through continuous observations of individual actions, but even more conclusively through certain generalizations. These amount to a discovery which I consider of the greatest moment to human society, and on which I shall briefly dwell. I got the first inkling of this astounding truth when I was still a very young man, but for many years I interpreted what I noted simply as coincidences. Namely, whenever either myself or a person to whom I was attached, or a cause to which I was devoted, was hurt by others in a particular way, which might be best popularly characterized as the most unfair imaginable, I experienced a singular and undefinable pain which, for want of a better term, I have qualified as "cosmic," and shortly thereafter, and invariably, those who had inflicted it came to grief. After many such cases I confided this to a number of friends, who had the opportunity to convince themselves of the truth of the theory which I have gradually formulated and which may be stated in the following few words:

Our bodies are of similar construction and exposed to the same external influences. This results in likeness of response and concordance of the general activities on which all our social and other rules and laws are based. We are automata entirely controlled by the forces of the medium being tossed about like corks on the surface of the water, but mistaking the resultant of the impulses from the outside for free will. The movements and other actions we perform are always life preservative and though seemingly quite independent from one another, we are connected by invisible links. So long as the organism is in perfect order it responds accurately to the agents that prompt it, but the moment that there is some derangement in any individual, his self-preservative power is impaired. Everybody understands, of course, that if one becomes deaf, has his eyesight weakened, or his limbs injured, the chances for his continued existence are lessened. But this is also true, and perhaps more so, of certain defects in the brain which deprive the automaton, more or less, of that vital quality and cause it to rush into destruction. A very sensitive and observant being, with his highly developed mechanism all intact, and acting with precision in obedience to the changing conditions of the environment, is endowed with a transcending mechanical sense, enabling him to evade perils too subtle to be directly perceived. When he comes in contact with others whose controlling organs are radically faulty, that sense asserts itself and he feels the "cosmic" pain. The truth of this has been borne out in hundreds of instances and I am inviting other students of nature to devote attention to this subject, believing that through combined and systematic effort results of incalculable value to the world will be attained.

The idea of constructing an automaton, to bear out my theory, presented itself to me early but I did not begin active work until 1893, when I started my wireless investigations. During the succeeding two or three years a number of automatic mechanisms, to be actuated from a distance, were constructed by me and exhibited to visitors in my laboratory. In 1896, however, I designed a complete machine capable of a multitude of operations, but the consummation of my labors was delayed until late in 1897. This machine was illustrated and described in my article in the *Century Magazine* of June, 1900, and other periodicals of that time and, when first shown in the beginning of 1898, it created a sensation such as no other invention of mine has ever produced. In November, 1898, a basic patent on the novel art was granted to me, but only after the Examiner-in-Chief had come to New York and witnessed the performance, for what I claimed seemed unbelievable. I remember that when later I called on an official in Washington, with a view of offering the invention to the Government, he burst out in laughter upon my telling him what I had accomplished. Nobody thought then that there was the faintest prospect of perfecting such a device. It is unfortunate that in this patent, following the advice of my attorneys, I indicated the control as being effected through the medium of a single circuit and a well-known form of detector, for the reason that I had not yet secured protection on my methods and apparatus for individualization. As a matter of fact, my boats were controlled through the joint action of several circuits and interference of every kind was excluded. Most generally I employed receiving circuits in the form of loops, including condensers, because the discharges of my high-tension transmitter ionized the air in the hall so that even a very small aerial would draw electricity from the surrounding atmosphere for hours. Just to give an idea, I found, for instance, that a bulb 12" in diameter, highly exhausted, and with one single terminal to which a short wire was attached, would deliver well on to one thousand successive flashes before all charge of the air in the laboratory was neutralized. The loop form of receiver was not sensitive to such a disturbance and it is curious to note that it is becoming popular at this late date. In reality it collects much less energy than the aerials or a long grounded wire, but it so happens that it does away with a number of defects inherent to the present wireless devices. In demonstrating my invention before audiences, the visitors were requested to ask any questions, however involved, and the automaton would answer them by signs. This was considered magic at that time but was extremely simple, for it was myself who gave the replies by means of the device.

At the same period another larger telautomatic boat was constructed, a photograph of which is shown in this number of the *Electrical Experimenter*. It was controlled by loops, having several turns placed in the hull, which was made entirely water-tight and capable of submergence. The apparatus was similar to that used in the first with the exception of certain special features I introduced as, for example, incandescent lamps which afforded a visible evidence of the proper functioning of the machine.

These automata, controlled within the range of vision of the operator, were, however, the first and rather crude steps in the evolution of the Art of Telautomatics as I had conceived it. The next logical improvement was its application to automatic mechanisms beyond the limits of vision and at great distance from the center of control, and I have ever since advocated their employment as instruments of warfare in preference to guns. The importance of this now seems to be recognized, if I am to judge from casual announcements through the press of achievements which are said to be extraordinary but contain no merit of novelty, whatever. In an imperfect manner it is practicable, with the existing wireless plants, to launch an aeroplane, have it follow a certain approximate course, and perform some operation at a distance of many hundreds of miles. A machine of this kind can also be mechanically controlled in several ways and I have no doubt that it may prove of some usefulness in war. But there are, to my best knowledge, no instrumentalities in existence today with which such an object could be accomplished in a precise manner. I have devoted years of study to this matter and have evolved means, making such and greater wonders easily realizable.

As stated on a previous occasion, when I was a student at college I conceived a flying machine quite unlike the present ones. The underlying principle was sound but could not be carried into practice for want of a prime-mover of sufficiently great activity. In recent years I have successfully solved this problem and am now planning aerial machines devoid to sustaining planes, ailerons, propellers and other external attachments, which will be capable of immense speeds and are very likely to furnish powerful arguments for peace in the near future. Such a machine, sustained and propelled entirely by reaction, is shown on page 108 and is supposed to be controlled either mechanically or by wireless energy. By installing proper plants it will be practicable to project a missile of this kind into the air and drop it almost on the very spot designated, which may be thousands of miles away. But we are not going to stop at this. Telautomata will be ultimately produced, capable of acting as if possessed of their own intelligence, and their advent will create a revolution. As early as 1898 I proposed to representatives of a large manufacturing concern the construction and public exhibition of an automotive carriage which, left to itself, would perform a great variety of operations involving something akin to judgement. But my proposal was deemed chimerical at that time and nothing came from it.

At present many of the ablest minds are trying to devise expedients for preventing a repetition of the awful conflict which is only theoretically ended and the duration and main issues of which I have correctly predicted in an article printed in the *Sun* of December 20, 1914. The proposed League is not a remedy but on the contrary, in the opinion of a number of competent men, may bring about results just the opposite. It is particularly regrettable that a punitive policy was adopted in framing the terms of peace, because a few years hence it will be possible for nations to fight without armies, ships or guns, by weapons far more terrible, to the destructive action and range of which there is virtually no limit. A city, at any distance whatsoever from the enemy, can be destroyed by him and no power on earth can stop him from doing so. If we want to avert an impending calamity and a state of things which may transform this globe into an inferno, we should push the development of flying machines and wireless transmission of energy without an instant's delay and with all the power and resources of the nation.